TEACHING THE FIRST CE
IN ENGLISH

Teaching the First Certificate in English

•

A Practical Guide for Teachers of English

by Larry Cole and Carolyn Jones

CASSELL

Cassell Publishers Limited
Artillery House
Artillery Row
London SW1P 1RT

British Library Cataloguing in Publication Data

Cole, Larry
Teaching the first certificate in English:
a practical guide for teachers of English

1. Non-English speaking students.
Curriculum subjects: English language.
Teaching
I. Title II. Jones, Carolyn
428.2′4′07

The Publishers are grateful to the following for permission to reproduce photographs:

Ace Photo Agency, pages 54, 106 and 109

and are grateful to
the University of Cambridge Local Examinations Syndicate
for permission to use extracts from the General Handbook, 1987

First published 1989

Designed by Vaughan Allen
Photoset in Plantin by Nene Phototypesetters Ltd, Northampton
Printed and bound by Mackays of Chatham Ltd

ISBN 0 304 31753 5

As we do not know the origins of all the ideas in this book, we are unable to acknowledge everyone by name but would like to thank all those who have contributed to it in any way.

Contents

INTRODUCTION

Who the book is for 1
What the book hopes to do 1
General description of the FCE examination:
- Basic ideas behind the Examination 1
- Contents of the Examination 3
- General marking procedure 4

Introduction to Chapters 1–5 – the Five Papers 5

CHAPTER 1 **PAPER 1 – READING COMPREHENSION**

General description 7
Contents of sections A and B 8
Breakdown of skills needed 11
Suggested classroom activities for Section A:
- Vocabulary: semantic fields or word families 13
- Vocabulary: collocation – adjective/noun relationships 17
- Vocabulary: collocation – phrasal verbs 20

Suggested classroom activities for Section B:
- Skimming 24
- Scanning 25
- Guessing unknown words 27
- Inferential reading 28
- Extracting central ideas and summarising 29
- Multiple-choice questions 30

CHAPTER 2 **PAPER 2 – COMPOSITION**

General description 33
Different types of composition 34
Breakdown of skills needed 35
Suggested classroom activities:
- Writing grammatically accurate sentences 36
- Punctuation 37
- Paragraphing 37
- Writing sentences to form a text 37
- Adapting style to the degree of formality 46
- Managing everyday functions 49
- Setting out a letter 50
- Writing extended narrative in the past tense 51
- Writing extended description 55
- Expressing opinions and organising them into a composition 56
- Choosing the right composition 59

CHAPTER 3 **PAPER 3 – USE OF ENGLISH**

General description 61
Contents of individual sections 62
Breakdown of skills needed 65
Suggested classroom activities:
Cloze texts 67
Sentence transformation 69
Vocabulary items 72
Incomplete dialogues 72
Writing a letter from notes 76
Paragraph writing and summarising 78

CHAPTER 4 **PAPER 4 – LISTENING COMPREHENSION**

General description 81
Contents of individual sections 81
Breakdown of skills needed 87
Suggested classroom activities:
Listening for gist 88
Listening for structures 90
Listening for specific factual information 91
Inferential listening 95
Predictive/Referential listening 97

CHAPTER 5 **PAPER 5 – THE INTERVIEW**

General description 100
Contents of individual sections 103
Breakdown of skills needed 103
Suggested classroom activities:
Warm-up phase 104
Describing a picture 105
Reading and discussing a short text 108
Participating in a communicative activity 110
The Oral examination as a whole 112
The Set Book option 112

Introduction

WHO THE BOOK IS FOR

The book is written for teachers of English as a foreign language in the UK and abroad, preparing intermediate-level secondary school or adult students for the First Certificate in English examination.

Many of the lesson ideas in the book require students to actively participate in the classroom. Pair and group work is thus a common feature of the book.

WHAT THE BOOK HOPES TO DO

There are two main objectives:

1 to break down each of the five papers into their component parts, analyse the language tasks required of candidates in each section and make practical suggestions for teachers to help their students acquire the relevant knowledge and practise the necessary skills to carry out the tasks successfully.

2 to 'demystify' the FCE examination by providing concise general information as to what it sets out to do and how it is marked.

From the above it is hoped that teachers will be given a realistic view of the Examination, as well as classroom ideas to help intermediate students meet the required standard. It is not our intention to provide a staged course across two or three years to guide Elementary students towards FCE pass level. Although some of the lesson suggestions may be used with Elementary or Lower-Intermediate students, most of our ideas are directed at teachers of students who are considered to have already reached an intermediate level of English. Some lessons may demand a higher linguistic level of students and these are marked ■.

GENERAL DESCRIPTION OF THE FCE EXAMINATION

Basic ideas behind the Examination

Before looking at what the Examination consists of, it is worth stating the basic ideas behind it. These are made explicit in the 'English as a Foreign Language General Handbook' which is published each year and contains details of the Examination and its general marking scheme.* We shall present the Handbook's ideas and comment on them with regard to our intentions in this book.

*This is available from UCLES, Syndicate Buildings, 1 Hills Road, Cambridge CB1 2EU, UK.

The introduction to the Handbook states that there are four different ideas behind the FCE syllabus. The first concerns classroom communicative approaches which the Cambridge Board seeks to encourage by means of the Examination. The second is the Board's intention to give greater weight to listening and speaking skills than in the past. Thirdly, the Board believes that listening and reading texts should be taken from authentic sources within a candidate's experience. Finally there is an attempt to avoid cultural bias in the Examination.

Let us now look more closely at the above ideas. For the purposes of this book, the first seems particularly important. It is clear that the Cambridge Board considers its Examinations as 'communicative', which loosely means using language as the basis of relationships between people so that when person A tells person B something through speaking or writing she hopes it will have some kind of effect. Communicative approaches, then, are essentially about interaction between people, and by suggesting these are encouraged by the Examination, the Board is making a clear policy statement that it wishes to see more communicative approaches in classes preparing for its Examinations. Thus, methodology in some countries and classrooms where students sit in rows and listen to the teacher, acting only on the teacher's instructions and working mostly as individuals in isolation from or in competition with each other is actively *discouraged* by the Examinations Board: it is not considered good teaching or sound preparation for the Examination.* But the Board explicitly hopes that prospective candidates will learn to work communicatively. Thus, it becomes of paramount importance that it is not just *what* they learn which matters but *how* they learn it.

Most of the teaching suggestions in this book reflect this thinking. Students are asked throughout the book to work in twos, threes, fours and small groups. They are often expected to discuss vocabulary and grammatical points with each other and the teacher. This means the teacher listens to what *they* have to say: perhaps asking why they think the answer they have chosen is correct; asking why they have written something in one way rather than another; perhaps even consulting them as to how they would like to go about working on a particular language area or exercise. Obviously, the teacher is the final arbiter of language correctness and decision making. But the stated intention of the Cambridge Examinations Board is that FCE students should be active not passive; thinking for themselves, not silently listening to the teacher do their thinking for them; working in pairs or groups, not sitting behind desks making little contact with other students in the class – generally working as hard as the teacher, if not harder, to explore the strange exciting territory of the English language.

The points made above reinforce this commitment to communicative methodologies. The Handbook's phrase 'to give greater weight to listening and speaking skills than in the past' assumes the pair/group/discussion emphasis just mentioned is already taking place wherever the English language is taught. This may not, in fact, be the case in all classrooms and all countries, especially in Examination

*Obviously, some teachers still have to teach in such situations, and they will, perhaps, have to adapt some of the ideas in this book to their own circumstances.

preparation classes which often tend to be regarded as 'special' classes doing mysteriously 'special' work. According to the Handbook, the Cambridge Board wishes FCE classes to be regarded as normal classes of students who just happen to be taking an examination at the end of their course. We would be pleased if, as a result of this book, attitudes generally become closer to the way Cambridge envisages them and teachers are helped in growing confident to try out the kinds of methods recommended in the Board's General Handbook.

We also welcome the Board's intention to avoid cultural bias in the examination. However, we would question whether it has been achieved, or even if it is a realistic goal. How far, in fact, can language ever be separated from the culture and society of which it is a part? The First Certificate examination is set in England by English-speaking people, and thus inevitably makes assumptions about life and society which may be unfamiliar to students from non-English speaking cultures, especially non-European ones. The texts presented in Section B of the Reading Comprehension paper, for example, are often about subjects of interest to many English-speaking people, but with possibly little meaning or relevance, let alone interest, to, eg, Arabic or Chinese candidates who are thus at a disadvantage that is not directly linguistic. This is an important area that teachers should be aware of.

Associated areas beyond the purely linguistic are those of the intellectual and imaginative demands made on candidates. Once again the texts in Section B of the Reading Comprehension paper assume a certain level of intelligence: logical and inferential thinking is tested as well as comprehension of factual information. And without imagination candidates can make little headway with the Composition paper. With regard to these aspects, however, we provide ideas which may be of help in approaching the Examination.

Contents of the Examination

A clear, concise statement of this occurs in the 'Regulations For 1987'*:

FIRST CERTIFICATE IN ENGLISH

The First Certificate represents a general standard of competence in English at an intermediate level and as an effective basis for further study. It has widespread recognition in commerce and industry, e.g. for public contact or secretarial work in banking, airlines, catering etc., and in individual university faculties, polytechnics and other institutions.

Certificates are awarded in three grades, A, B and C on the aggregate of marks gained in the five compulsory papers indicated below, with results also in two failing grades D and E.

PAPER 1 **Reading Comprehension** (1 hour) 40 marks

A 25 multiple-choice questions designed to test vocabulary and formal grammatical control, in sentence contexts

*Also available from UCLES, Syndicate Buildings, 1 Hills Road, Cambridge CB1 2EU, UK.

B 15 multiple-choice questions based on three or more texts, designed to test comprehension of gist or detailed content
(The initial mark weighting in Section A is one mark, and in Section B two marks, for each item)

PAPER 2 **Composition** (1½ hours) 40 marks

Two compositions from a choice of descriptive, narrative or discursive topics, including one based on the books listed on page 7
Assessment is based on organisation and clarity of content, accuracy of grammatical control, fluency and range of expression

PAPER 3 **Use of English** (2 hours) 40 marks

A Open-completion or transformation items designed to test active control of the language at an appropriate communicative level
B Directed writing exercise to test ability to interpret and present information

PAPER 4 **Listening Comprehension** (approx. 30 minutes) 20 marks

Questions of varying type (selection, re-ordering, blank-filling etc.) to test accurate understanding of spoken English, based on recorded material

PAPER 5 **Interview** (approx. 15 minutes) 40 marks

Based on a picture stimulus, and related passages and other material. The interview may, optionally, be based partly on one of the books listed on page 7, and be conducted, also optionally, with individual candidates or in groups of two or three.

Assessment is based on fluency and grammatical accuracy, pronunciation (individual sounds, and stress and linking of phrases), communicative ability and vocabulary.

General marking procedure

In the section on 'Examination Processing' the Handbook says it wishes to strike a balance between the strengths and limitations of various accepted testing formats. The aim is to correlate marks between the five papers to produce an all-over grading for each candidate.

Two points about the First Certificate marking procedure are made by this. The first concerns objective and subjective testing procedures. The objective tests, where there is only one correct answer (Paper 1 – Reading Comprehension and Paper 4 – Listening Comprehension), are computer processed. The subjective tests (Paper 2 – Composition and Paper 5 – Interview) depend on marks awarded for performances in various communicative activities and are thus necessarily marked subjectively. The Board says it regards Paper 3 (The Use of English) as a mixture of both objective and subjective formats, which are used about equally in the overall marking system. The second point states that the final mark is awarded on the relationship between papers: the candidate is thus expected to have an all-round ability in the areas tested by the examination. It is a system of checks and balances: a candidate's performance in one part of the examination is checked against that in other parts before a final assessment is arrived at. Thus, student questions of the type, *'If I pass the Composition paper, the Reading Comprehension and the Interview but fail the other two, will I pass overall?'* have little meaning in reality. Each paper is considered as existing not in isolation but as dependent on and contributing to the others, and the examination should be viewed as a whole.

The Board states in the General Handbook that research is still being carried out into the overall reliability of the examination, but that the evidence so far suggests the current mode of testing and marking may generally be considered reliable and satisfactory.

INTRODUCTION TO CHAPTERS 1–5 – THE FIVE PAPERS

The second section of the book is organised into five chapters, each dealing with one paper. Each chapter begins with an overall description of the paper under consideration. This makes reference to what the paper has contained since 1984 when the Examination assumed its current form. There are, of course, no hard-and-fast rules as to the detailed content of any of the papers: one of the main points about examinations is their inbuilt quality of unpredictability. There can, however, be general explanations of the types of questions candidates may anticipate, and this is what we attempt to give in this section.

A breakdown of the paper into its constituent parts follows. Clearly, this varies from paper to paper: the Use of English paper, for instance, most readily lends itself to this analysis of sub-sections, although the format is also used with the other papers. In doing this we give examples of the kinds of questions that have been set so that teachers will be clear about the possible examination tasks their students may be asked to perform.

The remainder of each chapter is the central focus of the book. We go back over each section, analyse a cross-section of examples, list, where possible, discrete language items tested and make practical classroom suggestions whereby teachers can help students master the skills and grammatical points necessary for successful completion of the tasks. Concentration is on what teachers can do with more classes, and how this can be done. We are short on 'whys' and 'wherefores', as this book is practical rather than theoretical. Although at times the book may read like a shopping list of 'you can do's, any disadvantages of this approach are outweighed by the advantages of simplicity, clarity and usability. Detailed lesson plans are not provided, merely guidelines as to how teachers may go about teaching what we put before them. Nor is our list of suggestions meant to be exhaustive: we would like to encourage teachers to think of their own ideas and prepare their own materials. Because of this, we are deliberately eclectic and inconsistent in our approach to lesson presentation, sometimes providing teachers with more detailed material they can use in class with students, on other occasions merely making suggestion outlines for teachers as springboards for their imaginations. We do not claim that our ideas are particularly original, but they have all, however, been tried and tested in the classroom – FCE and otherwise – and adhere to the basic recommendations of the Handbook presented and discussed on pp1–3. Teachers are free to select, amend, extend and improve on our ideas.

As one might expect from the Board's reference to the interdependence of papers, there is much overlap of test items across the five papers. In order to avoid repetition, we make a particular lesson suggestion under the section of the Examination which we feel most strongly emphasises the language aspect being practised. Also, of course, many of our lesson ideas teach or practise more than one area. There is thus a certain amount of cross-referencing in the Classroom activities section of each chapter.

CHAPTER 1

Paper 1
Reading Comprehension

GENERAL DESCRIPTION

There are two sections to this paper, both using a multiple-choice format as the testing procedure. Section A contains 25 unconnected sentences with one word or short phrase omitted in each sentence. Sometimes two sentences are supplied in one test item. Candidates are asked to select the missing item from four alternatives given below each sentence or pair of sentences, only one of which is structurally and semantically correct. This is a test of both vocabulary awareness and grammatical control.

In Section B candidates are required to read three texts of connected English. After each of these there are from four to six multiple-choice questions with only one correct answer in each case. There is a maximum total of 15 multiple-choice test items to be answered in Section B.

The first two texts are usually of a literary nature. They are taken from books, or made to look as if they have been. Three basic types of text may comprise the first and second reading passages – an apparently factual, impersonal description of a place, a process, a sociological trend, etc; a personal narrative; or a real or simulated extract from a work of fiction written in the third person. Sometimes two different types of text are presented in the first two questions, at other times two of a similar kind, eg two impersonal descriptive passages. The third text is usually more practical in nature and may consist of a formal notice giving information or regulations. Sometimes more than one such text is presented – maybe three or four short extracts – and candidates are asked to make comparisons between them. It is not possible to be more specific about the type of passages chosen in Section B, as there is clearly a wide variety of written English styles and texts available for testing purposes.

In Section A each correct answer is awarded one mark, and in Section B two marks. No marks are deducted for wrong answers. Thus the final mark of 40 for this paper is worked out mathematically from the total possible aggregate of 55.

CONTENTS OF SECTIONS **A** AND **B**

Section A

The 25 sentences or pairs of sentences test a wide range of discrete language items. The following are the most frequently occurring areas:

VOCABULARY: SEMANTIC FIELDS OR WORD FAMILIES

This is the most common type of question in Section A. Candidates are asked to supply the correct noun, adjective or verb from the context. Three typical examples are as follows:

1 You should see your dentist regularly for ....
A a review **B** a control **C** an investigation **D** a check-up

2 First, boil some water in a .... and then add the potatoes.
A tray **B** dish **C** pan **D** tin

3 This antique is so rare that it is ....
A useless **B** worthless **C** priceless **D** valueless

The correct answer has to be chosen from four lexical items in the same word family. In Question 1 this could be called 'Testing/Supervising'; in Question 2 'Utensils'; in Question 3 'adjectives connected with financial assessment'. If the candidate did not already know the omitted vocabulary item, there is no way he could guess it or work it out. These types of test items are not dependent on adjoining words: eg in Question 2 you either know a pan is what you boil water in, or you don't. And, if in Question 3 he applied logic to deduce that both 'priceless' and 'valueless' meant, respectively, 'without price' and 'without value', he would still not be able to work out that the first actually meant 'beyond price' and had, in fact, an opposite meaning from the second.

VOCABULARY: COLLOCATION – ADJECTIVE + NOUN RELATIONSHIPS

This too is vocabulary based but more directly concerned with word relationships. A simple definition of 'collocation' is words that go together to form a unit. Sometimes there is only one word in English which 'collocates' with another, at other times a few words 'fit' but one is usually felt to 'fit' better than the others. An example of the latter occurs in the following:

After her husband left her she was so upset she nearly died of a .... heart.

'Troubled', 'heavy' and 'grieving' could possibly go before 'heart' here and could be regarded as weak collocations. However, the word which most people would surely supply is 'broken' – 'to die of a broken heart' being a phrase that has been used so often as to become a cliché. Collocations where only one word is possible include numerous idiomatic expressions: 'a rainy day' in 'saving up for a rainy day', 'a red herring' in 'That's just a red herring – stick to the point' and so on. Three typical examples are as follows:

1 From my house there is a good .... of the sea.
A picture **B** sight **C** vision **D** view

2 The chairman has not yet reached a .... decision on the future of the organisation.
A solid **B** firm **C** strong **D** heavy

3 The farmers had a very good crop of .... last year.
A wheat **B** grass **C** eggs **D** milk

The correct choice of the missing words here depends largely on candidates' knowledge of word relationships. For example, there is no reason why 'sight' could not be correct in Question 1 or 'strong' in Question 2, except that a 'good sight of the sea' and a 'strong decision' are not correct English – at least in the contexts presented in these sentences.

VOCABULARY: COLLOCATION – PHRASAL VERBS

Phrasal and prepositional verbs are also often tested. By this we mean verbs like 'get' which may be followed by numerous prepositions or phrases such as 'in', 'on', 'at', 'away with', 'by', and 'on top of'. Candidates may either be given the verb and have to choose the correct prepositional phrase, or the other way round. Three typical examples are as follows:

1 John looked .... to see who had come into the room.
A for **B** after **C** up **D** at

2 The library had to .... down on the number of books it bought.
A get **B** turn **C** cut **D** put

3 That chair doesn't fit .... with the rest of the furniture.
A up **B** in **C** beside **D** on

Phrasal verb forms are also often tested in the Use of English paper. See pp62–3.

GRAMMATICAL CONTROL

Here candidates are tested on their understanding of grammatical structure such as conditionals, passives, and reported speech. The object here may be to determine if candidates know the correct verb form to supply – eg past participle, gerund, infinitive, – or the correct conjunction, preposition or adverb. Three typical examples are as follows:

1 If we had known you were ill, we .... to see you.
A have come **B** will come **C** would come **D** would have come

2 They completed the work .... a month.
A for **B** in **C** by **D** before

3 Students are requested .... in the library.
A not talking **B** don't talk **C** not to talk **D** from talking.

This type of test item occurs less frequently than types 1, 2 and 3 – perhaps because grammatical ability is tested more comprehensively in the Composition and Use of English papers.

VOCABULARY: PARTS OF SPEECH

Less frequently candidates are given the same word in its different conjugational forms – verb, noun, adjective, adverb – and asked to choose the correct form in the context. Three typical examples are as follows:

1 The government is constantly looking for ways to .... costs.
A reduce **B** reduced **C** reducing **D** reduction

2 My uncle was very shocked when his boss dismissed him, particularly as he had been an .... of the company for 30 years.
A employment **B** employer **C** employ **D** employee

3 Calm down! Don't be so ....!
A child **B** childhood **C** childlike **D** childish

This type of test item is perhaps less arbitrary than any of the others. In number 1 candidates might at least be expected to recognise the correct part of speech is not D, a noun, and in 3, the answer is not A or B, also nouns.

Most, if not all of the language items tested in Section A fall into one of the above categories. One important point is that candidates are being tested on more than just one missing word in a sentence. In example 3 of the 'Semantic fields or Word families' section and example 3 of the 'Vocabulary: Parts of speech' section, for instance, if candidates do not know the meanings of 'rare' and 'calm down', respectively, they cannot be expected to choose the correct item from the four alternatives.

Section B

This section contains three texts, each followed by between four and six multiple choice questions, totalling fifteen. There are four basic types of text which can appear on this paper. The texts in the first two questions are usually chosen from the following written styles:

1 A text taken from a real or simulated work of fiction written in the third person. There are obviously as many variations as there are books to choose from. Sources are not cited in the papers, but a typical example could be a narrative about:

a character returning to a place where he lived as a child / a character arriving home early in the morning / a character beginning a new job abroad.

2 A personal account of an experience. This is a first-person narrative about something that happened to the writer. Subject areas could be:

> an escape from a sinking ship / a climb up one of the world's highest mountains / an arrival in a foreign country.

3 A factual, impersonal description of a place, a process or a sociological trend, for example:

> fishing / spiders / trade unions / Heathrow Airport / jogging for health / film review.

The third and final question is usually based on the following:

4 A practical text or texts, often giving information, rules or regulations, instructions of some kind. Some examples might be:

> a holiday competition entry form / travel hints for Australia with prices / fresh vegetables – their comparative nutritive contents / how to apply for a passport / four book descriptions.

As stated in the General description of the paper, the testing format is multiple-choice. Each gives four possible alternatives – one of which is correct, three of which act as distractors. The grammatical structure of the test item is either a direct question as in:

Where was John's father's caravan?

- **A** on the edge of Swineford
- **B** near the church in Swineford
- **C** in a small town on a bus route from Swineford
- **D** in the countryside a few miles from Swineford

or an unfinished sentence as in:

The girl began to hesitate as she was talking to her father because ....

- **A** he didn't believe her.
- **B** he made her feel uncomfortable.
- **C** he became very angry.
- **D** he was not behaving as she thought he would.

BREAKDOWN OF SKILLS NEEDED

Section A

From the analysis of language aspects tested in Section A, it is clear that students preparing for this paper need to acquire a fairly large vocabulary, both active and passive, in major areas: Semantic fields or word families, Collocation – adjective/noun relationships, and Collocation – phrasal verbs.

Students need a large passive vocabulary to understand the information in the sentences presented to them and an active vocabulary to supply the missing word. Four of the five types of test item identified have been lexical. To a lesser extent structural knowledge is also examined, but as the test items differ little from those in the Use of English, suggestions for grammar and structure practice are made in that section and in the Composition section rather than here.

Section B

In order to answer questions of the type listed on pp10–11 students need to be familiar with many different styles of written English. The best way of preparing for Paper 1 Section B is to read as much as possible.

However, students often create difficulties for themselves in reading. Perhaps the most common ways they do this are the following:

- They lose sight of the general meaning of a passage by paying too much attention to detail in the early stages.
- Once they have grasped the general meaning, they experience difficulty in discriminating between important and less important information.
- They lose confidence when confronted by unknown words and expressions.
- They have difficulty understanding ideas which are implied rather than overtly stated.
- They have problems with extracting and summarising the central idea(s) of a text.
- Where multiple choice is used as a testing format as in the FCE examination, they find this procedure unfamiliar and off-putting.

We therefore suggest that students need to practise the following skills:

- Skimming passages – reading quickly in order to get the gist or general idea.
- Scanning passages in order to find specific information.
- Guessing unknown words from their context.
- Inferential reading – finding information which is not clearly stated, and drawing conclusions from separate pieces of information; and being sensitive to the writer's attitude and the implications of what is said.
- Reading for central or important ideas, and summarising them.
- Practising answering multiple-choice questions.

SUGGESTED CLASSROOM ACTIVITIES FOR SECTION A

Vocabulary – semantic fields or word families

1 Students alone or in twos or threes make lists of

eg: Things you can buy in a chemist's / Things you need for a holiday by the sea / Things you find in a kitchen

There could be a number of different lists, and individuals, pairs or small groups are given four or five minutes to work on a list before passing it to another student or other students who, in turn, pass theirs on to someone else. After another five minutes the lists get passed on again. Each list thus keeps moving around the class, and the exercise gets more challenging when students must think of new objects to add to already fairly full and comprehensive lists. Dictionaries may be referred to. After about 25 minutes the class is brought together and some or all of the word lists written on the board.

2 The teacher draws a circle on the board with the name of a word family in the centre, and lines leading off it like a spider's legs

eg:

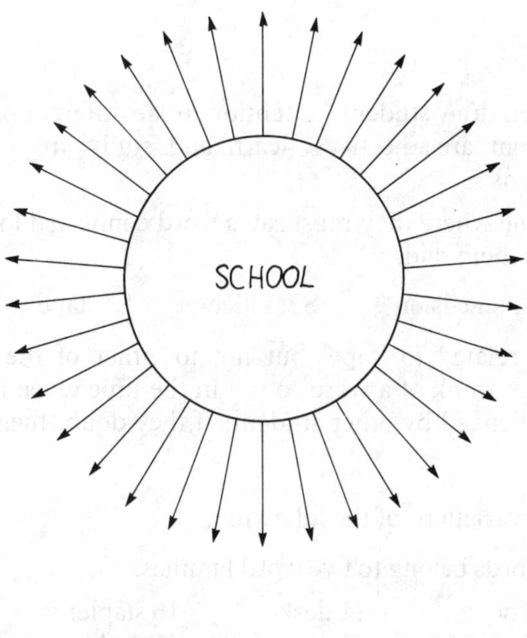

Students then think of as many words as possible that could go in the Word Family 'School'. They do this in pairs and/or come out to the board and write them at the end of the lines. Some kind of team game can be developed. The finished product could look something like this:

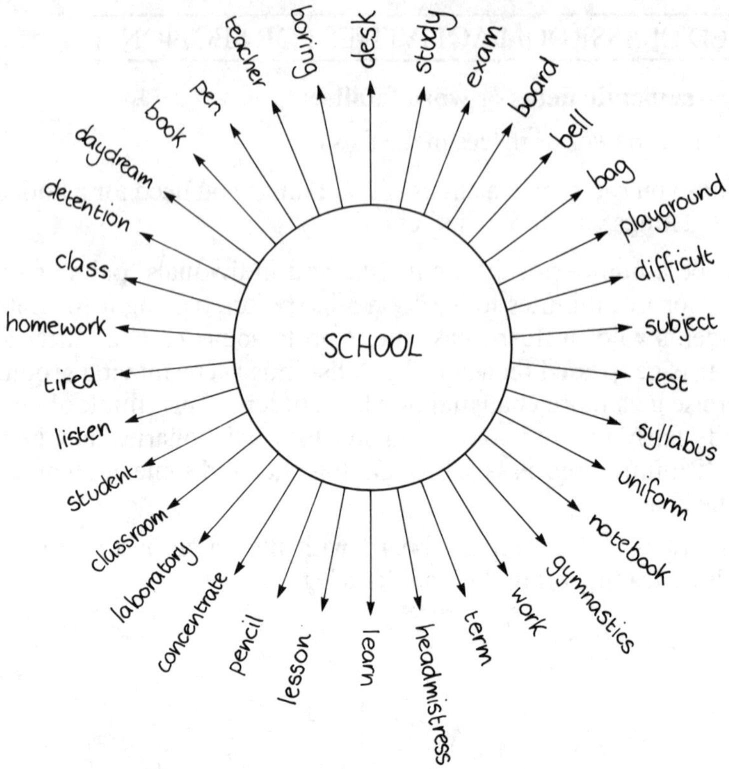

The teacher can then draw students' attention to the different parts of speech – how 'boring' and 'different' are adjectives, 'learn' and 'study' are verbs, and most of the other words are nouns.

3 Students play a game where they must say a word connected to the one the student immediately before them said.

eg: S1: television S2: video S3: tape S4: measure

Here 'measure' is related to 'tape' but not to either of the two earlier words. Students who do not think of a word to say in the time given are out of the game. Words may be challenged by other students if they doubt their relationship to the previous word.

4 Students can be set variations of the following:

The following 50 words belong to five word families:

1 racket	6 boot	11 desk	16 stapler	21 score
2 sink	7 wheel	12 oven	17 dashboard	22 paper clip
3 ignition	8 pitch	13 tie	18 match	23 computer
4 fridge	9 shorts	14 pants	19 bin	24 ring
5 suit	10 typewriter	15 tyre	20 indicator	25 ribbon

26 track
27 drawers
28 draw
29 saucepan
30 filofax
31 bat
32 game
33 grill
34 umpire
35 belt
36 instructor
37 seat
38 club
39 licence
40 buckle
41 tap
42 bonnet
43 windscreen
44 scarf
45 rubber
46 photocopier
47 washing machine
48 clutch
49 court
50 ground

Find the five families and put each word into the family it belongs to. Call your families either 'Things you find in...............' or 'Things you associate with...............' Some words belong to more than one family.

The class divides into five pairs of groups. Each group takes a different family and writes a brief description of what each word in the family is used for. The name is omitted from the definition,

eg: pen – It's something people write with *or* You write with it. It has ink in it.

Each group takes it in turns to read one of its definitions to the class. The other students guess the word from the description.

5 Word Family Puzzles of the kind often found in puzzle books are also useful – and fun into the bargain. Here is an example:

Students look at the clues and see if they can find 19 household items hidden in the square. We have done two to start with.

L	S	H	D	O	O	R	M	A	T	M	O
A	O	**C**	**U**	**R**	**T**	**A**	**I**	**N**	**S**	I	T
N	F	H	E	A	T	E	R	C	B	R	E
N	A	I	**K**	E	Y	R	R	X	P	O	C
E	B	V	**N**	A	K	W	O	V	E	N	T
E	S	C	**I**	S	S	O	R	S	J	R	A
V	A	D	**F**	G	S	H	E	L	F	C	R
C	U	P	**E**	N	C	I	L	Q	U	L	R
O	C	R	B	U	U	V	A	S	E	O	E
O	E	S	E	P	P	S	M	H	G	C	O
L	R	A	D	I	O	N	P	C	L	K	E
D	R	N	U	A	E	L	N	G	Y	N	L

CLUES

Across

You open the door with it
You cut paper with them
You write with it
You listen to it
You close them at night
You put books on it
You cook in it
You switch it on to keep warm
You put flowers in it
You wipe your feet on it

Down

You look in it
You drink from it
You sleep in it
You sit on it
You tell the time from it
You put your cup on it
You use it to see in the dark
You use it after you have washed your clothes
You cut food with it

6 Students can work on an 'Odd Word Out' line game of this kind: There are five words beside each number below. All belong to the same word family except one. Find the family four belong to, then find four other words which go into a family with the Odd Words Out. Here is an example:

1 counter sun stock commodity customer
2 pillow beach sea sand tan
3 orange apple potato peach strawberry
4 drill filling injection waiting room stethoscope

The Odd Word Out in 1 is 'sun', so the students would find 4 other 'weather' words to go with it, eg rain, snow, hail, thunder, etc.

The next stage is for students to create their own lines to give to other students to answer.

7 ■ Most texts are about a particular theme or themes. For instance, a text entitled 'Drunken drivers should receive heavier punishments' might reasonably be expected to contain words relating to three subject areas – drunkenness, cars/driving and punishments which can be inflicted by the legal system. Students can be given the title of the text and asked to predict the words which might occur in it. In the case of the above, they can be divided into three groups with each group given one of the themes to work on. After 10 or 15 minutes the lists are written on the board with attention paid to the meanings of the various words. Finally, the text is read and discussion takes place as to how close the predictions were to the vocabulary in the actual passage. A revised list might well be made of the 'family' words in the text which the students had not previously thought of.

8 ■ The class is divided into two groups. Students in each group are given a different completed crossword with all the words belonging to the same family. Their task is to make up a clue for each word for the other group to guess. For instance, group A would be given a 'Clothes' crossword, part of which might look like this:

while group B is given a completed crossword about 'Sport'. Both groups work out sets of clues for their crossword. Group A's clues might look like this:

Across	**Down**
1. Worn for warmth in winter	2. Its length varies according to fashion
4. It protects you from the rain	3. Trousers in the USA, underwear in the UK
5. Fashion accessory	4. An old piece of cloth
6. Your tie is worn over this	

When each group have agreed on and written their clues, students in each group are given the incomplete version of the other group's crossword. Groups take it in turns to ask for clues and complete their crosswords.

Vocabulary – collocation – adjective/noun relationships

1 ■ Students are given a table with adjectives on the left and nouns on the right. Most of the adjectives can be put before only one of the nouns, although a few 'fit' two or even three. The students' task is to sort out which adjective goes with which noun or nouns. They could work in pairs or small groups to do this. Here is an example of some fairly difficult material which could be used in this way:

A light	1 hands
B open	2 film
C sweet	3 homework
D dirty	4 dress
E late	5 break
F stained	6 door
G easy	7 standard of living
H social	8 front
I healthy	9 taste
J pretty	10 explanation
K high	11 arrival
L slow	12 meal
M exciting	13 entrance
N brave	14 tooth
O bad	15 train
P clear	16 helping
Q lucky	17 climber
R narrow	18 joke
S cold	19 appetite
T generous	20 glass

After 30 minutes or so the students discuss their results with each other and the teacher who monitors and corrects.

An extension or reinforcement of this is for students to compose, say, 10 to 12 Section A test items to give each other – based on the collocations in this table. For example, after they know 'late arrival' is correct, a possible test item would be:

> When he came 10 minutes late for the lesson Peter apologised to his teacher for his late .... **A** entrance **B** coming **C** arrival **D** appearance

The three incorrect words or 'distractors' should be of the same part of speech as the missing word, and as near as possible to it in meaning. By setting questions as well as answering them, students are learning how to anticipate the kinds of sentences which might come up in the examination. Teachers help and correct students' grammar before pairs or groups of students answer each other's test sentences.

2 ■ Students answer selected questions based on collocation from either past papers or practice books. After they know the correct answer, they are asked to work in pairs or groups to find a word which 'collocates' with each of the distractors, then make further test items for fellow students to answer. The following test item which we have already seen is a good example:

> From my house there is a good .... of the sea.
> **A** picture **B** sight **C** vision **D** view

After finding the correct answer – **D** view – groups of students take each of the three distractors and place appropriate qualifiers before or after them. Dictionaries will almost certainly be needed to do this.

A	B	C
a beautiful picture *clear* *good* a picture of health *happiness*	bad (eye) sight *good* a beautiful sight *horrible* a sight for sore eyes	good vision *poor*

Two possible test items from the above would be:

> Mary was lucky enough to have such good .... that she could see the number on the bus from half a mile away.
>
> **A** sight **B** picture **C** view **D** looks
>
> I don't have a .... picture of what it is exactly you want me to do.
>
> **A** clear **B** healthy **C** happy **D** beautiful

The students then give their test items to classmates to answer.

3 ■ Cloze-type or gap-filling exercises of all kinds are also useful for collocation work, especially in teaching students common idiomatic expressions. After sensitising students to collocation, by getting them to do the above tasks and giving them practice with texts where every 7th or 8th word is blanked out, the teacher then divides the class into groups and asks each group to

- **a** find a text which interests them, is of a suitable length and at an appropriate level
- **b** list adjective/noun examples in the text and common idiomatic expressions
- **c** blank out suitable words in collocational relationships.

For example, in a text beginning: 'This week Bob Johnson makes his debut as a radio presenter and picks some of his favourite records from the 1960s', 'makes' and 'debut', 'radio' and 'presenter', 'picks', 'favourite' and 'records' all respectively collocate, and a possible blanked version might read:

> This week Bob Johnson (1)............... his debut as a radio (2)............... and picks some of his (3)............... records from the 1960s.

Students then exchange their gapped texts and try to complete. Ideally some collocations would be 'strong' ('makes' and 'favourite' above) and others 'weak' ('presenter'). 'Weak' collocations do not usually occur in the examination but are good for stimulating thought and discussion about the parameters of English. Students then return their completed versions to the group who set it for them. Discussion ensues. Finally, the teacher brings the class together and acts as final arbiter of correctness.

4 The teacher has a completed text. If there are 30 words in the text, the numbers 1 to 30 are written on the board.

The teacher then gives the student a title for the text and students work in groups in a class team game, calling out individual words they think fit. Each group gets a point for a correct word. If a group says 'the' and there are four 'the's in the text, all four are written in by the teacher and the group scores four points. If there is only one 'woman', the teacher writes 'woman' in the number equivalent where it comes in the text and the group scores one point.

Vocabulary: collocation – phrasal verbs

1 A phrasal verb is chosen and all the various prepositional phrases which can follow it are given in list form. Exercise-type practice with dictionaries follows. An example of this is to take the verb 'look' and provide students with practice and exploration of its use with a number of prepositions, leading from the controlled to the relatively free. A table such as the following overleaf can be given:

Verb	Phrasal verb	Example
Look	look for	I'm looking for my purse. I don't remember where I put it.
	look at	I'm looking at this page. It's not a big problem. It depends how you look at it.
	look forward to	I'm looking forward to seeing you again.
	look in	Look in and say hello on your way home.
	look up	Look up any words you don't know in your dictionary.
	look over	Can you look over my homework before I give it in.
	look on	Many people look on this government as the answer to their problems.
	look into	Leave the matter with me – I'll look into it.

Other common verbs of this kind such as 'get' and 'take' also lend themselves to this treatment.

Students are then given exercises as the following to test their comprehension and control of the phrasal verb.

A Put one word in each blank space using the verbs above:

- **a** Look .... this time of your life as a preparation for the future.
- **b** Can you look .... at the Post Office when you pass by and get me a stamp?
- **c** I looked .... the new proposal, and it seems to be all right.
- **d** You'll have to look .... his number in the phone book.
- **e** I hate work! I'm really looking .... to the weekend.
- **f** Look .... it this way. If you don't try, you won't succeed.

B Replace the italicised word with an appropriate form of 'look':

- **a** I think we'll have to *investigate* the reasons for your son's depression, Mrs Smith.

b Can you *try to find* my umbrella in the car please?
c I've *checked* the new flat to make sure everything is all right.
d The new job will be great. I *see* it as an important move.
e I'll have to *consult* your record in my files.

C Make a response to the following sentences, using the words in brackets and the appropriate form of 'look':

a What does this word mean? (dictionary)
b Have you seen Susan's new baby? (this evening/after work)
c I think I've made a lot of typing errors in this letter (you'd better/boss)
d Please write soon (hear your news)
e My camera's broken (let me ....)
f I've lost the book John lent me (if I were you/he arrives)

Alternatively, phrasal verbs can be taught according to their functional areas. In the examples provided here the function is 'telephoning':

2 TELEPHONING 1

Use these phrasal verbs in the sentences below:

put down / ring off / speak up / hang up on / get through (to) /
pick up / hold on / ring back / look up / put someone through (to)

a He was very rude to her, so she .... him.
b I couldn't hear him so I asked him to ....
c If you can't .... her, ask the operator to help you.
d She wasn't in, so I had to .... again later.
e Because I was feeling so angry with what he said, I ....
f When I'd finished talking, I .... the receiver.
g .... a minute, I'll try to find her for you.
h I got the wrong number. I'd better .... in the directory again.

TELEPHONING 2

Fill in the blanks:

Every time I try to .... to Harry in his office I have problems. The receptionist always tells me that I've got the wrong number and .... me. When I .... she tells me to .... and then takes ages to .... his office. If he finally .... the receiver I usually can't hear him clearly and have to ask him to .... More often than not, I .... with the feeling that I haven't achieved anything at all!

Another way of arranging phrasal verbs is according to theme. In the material provided here the subject of 'Health' is explored. Students are first asked to link an illness expression with its definition before going on to do some progressively demanding exercises.

3 HEALTH I

Look at the list on the left and find the definition or expression which means the same from the list on the right:

1	He *came round* very quickly after his operation.	**A**	make you depressed
2	Feeling unwell all the time can *get you down*.	**B**	recover from
3	You'll soon *be up and about* again.	**C**	faint, lose consciousness
4	It took her a year to fully *get over* her illness.	**D**	regain consciousness
5	In hot, crowded places people sometimes *pass out*.	**E**	get out of bed and be active

HEALTH 2

Substitute a phrasal verb for the italicised words:

a It takes two weeks for a child to *recover from* measles.
b The disco was so hot and crowded that I *fainted*.
c As soon as she'd had the baby, she was *out of bed* and back to normal.
d He *recovered consciousness* when he heard his favourite singer on the radio.
e City life can *make you depressed*.

HEALTH 3

Answer these questions using a phrasal verb:

a Why do a lot of people prefer to live in the country?
b How long does influenza usually last?
c What can happen to people who find the atmosphere too hot and oppressive?
d What happens to you immediately after an operation?

A large number of thematic areas lend themselves to this kind of treatment. The topic 'Weather' often features the following phrasal verbs:

brighten up / cloud over / clear up / pour down / freeze up

'Crime' includes:

> break into / hold up / let off / track down / get off / beat up / turn in / make off.

There are many more.

4 Similar material to any of the above can be prepared with the preposition as the focus rather than the verb, function or topic area. For instance, the preposition 'down' could be the focus of the work, and a selection of common verbs which collocate with 'down': get down / turn down / slow down / run down / bring down / take down – are then practised in any of the ways shown above.

5 However phrasal verbs are categorised – whether by verbs, prepositions or themes – students can be given two sets of cards, one set with the verbs on, the other set with their dictionary definitions. The cards are placed face up on a table, and the students' task is to match pairs of cards. For instance, on the table:

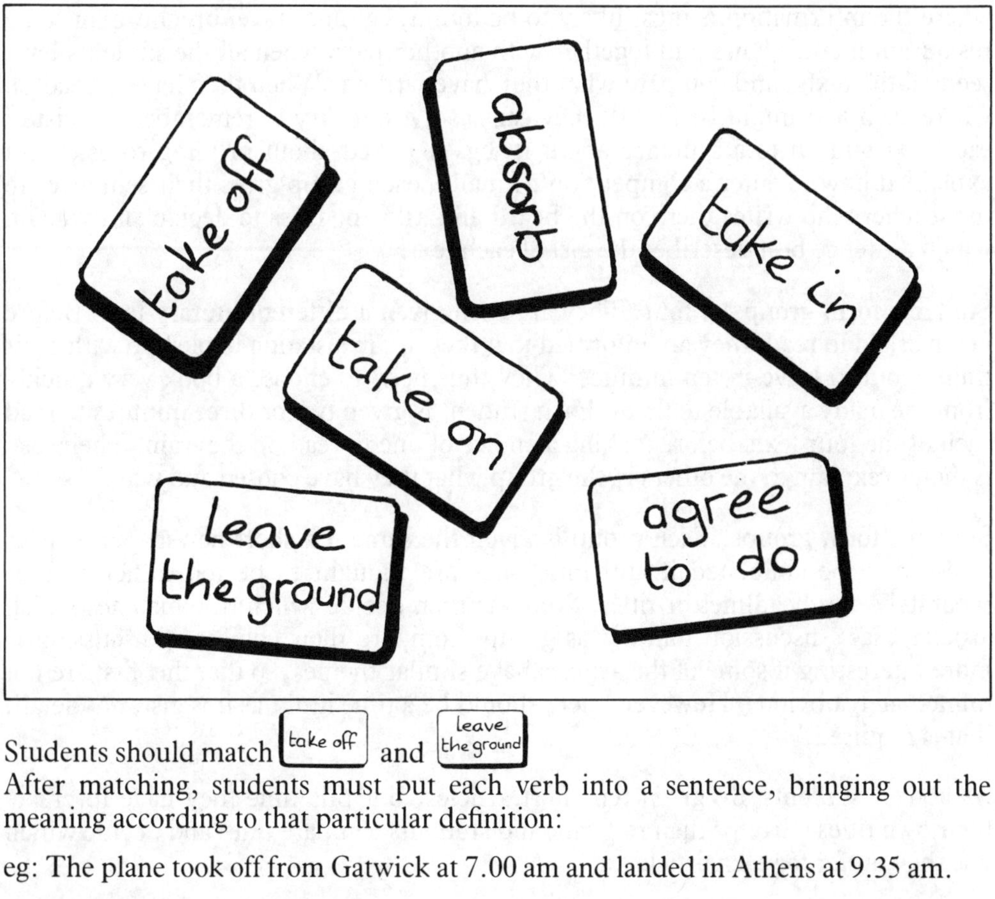

Students should match [take off] and [leave the ground]

After matching, students must put each verb into a sentence, bringing out the meaning according to that particular definition:

eg: The plane took off from Gatwick at 7.00 am and landed in Athens at 9.35 am.

SUGGESTED CLASSROOM ACTIVITIES FOR SECTION B

Skimming

1 All the students read the same text for two minutes, then turn it over. They each write down the first five words that come into their minds about the contents of the text they have read. They then compare their list with their partner's and discuss which words best indicate what the text is about. Each pair produces a new list of five from the ten words that they have between them. Pairs then join together with another pair and the process is repeated. Finally, each group of four reports to the class the five words they have decided on, and the teacher writes all the words on the board. The class then discuss and vote on which five words best summarise the feeling of the text, giving their reasons.

2 A selection of texts is passed around the class, each one with a number on the back for easy checking. When a pair receives a text they discuss and then write down the kind of article or book they think the extract comes from, eg 'a book of gardening advice' or 'a novel set in Africa'. In the case of more practical texts they write down where the information is most likely to be found, eg 'in a travel brochure' or 'on a restaurant menu'. Pairs join together with another pair, when all the students have seen all the texts, and compare what they have written. When they have agreed on where each text might be found, they can, as a group, try to remember the gist of each text and write a sentence about it, eg 'It talked about pruning roses' or 'It explained how to enter a competition'. Finally, each group gives their sentences to the teacher who writes them on the board and asks the class to decide and vote on which sentence best describes the gist of each text.

3 Students form groups of four. They are each given a different literary text. Before being asked to read, they are informed that they are in a station bookshop with their train about to leave in ten minutes. They thus need to choose a book very quickly from the many available to them. Each student is given two or three minutes to read each of the four texts before making a choice of one to read on the train. Their task is then to explain to the others in the group what they have chosen and why.

4 Students form groups. Each group is given the same ten short newspaper articles (these may be simulated if authentic ones are thought to be too difficult) and, separately, ten headlines or titles. Students then decide which title matches which article. Class discussion follows, as groups compare their choices. (Discussion is more interesting if some of the articles have similar themes, so that the 'fits' are not immediately obvious. However, there should be a time limit, as it is gist, not detail, that is required.)

5 As above, students are given ten short articles, but this time they have to create their own titles. Groups then re-form, and students compare titles and decide which one they prefer for each article.

6 Students form groups of three. Each group is given ten texts of different types – the same ten texts to each group, each one with a number in the corner. The teacher calls out 'Find a text which................' and the first group to call out the number of the correct text wins a point.

eg: Find a text which mentions London / describes an accident / reviews a play / was set in the last century / tells you how to keep fit / gives prices of air travel to India / etc

Groups can then make up their own 'Find a text which................' tasks, as above, for other groups to answer – each group takes it in turns to call and the other groups compete to find the text referred to and call out the appropriate number. The teacher awards points on the board for the quickest. The class can dispute if they think the wrong text has been selected.

Scanning

1 Pairs of students are all given the same three or four factual texts based on the same theme. These themes could be food, work, education or tourist information. They can then work through the following types of activity in any order:

- How many names of people can you find?
  How many names of places can you find?
- Write down as many words connected with food/work/school/entertainment as you can find.
- Locate the lines in which specific information can be found about cooking mushrooms/attending a job interview/taking examinations/what to do in London after midnight.
- Decide if the following information is true or false according to the text: The best apples can be found in Worcester. / Experience is more important than qualifications. / All students stay at school until they are eighteen. / Trains in London stop running at 1.00 am.

Students should correct statements they consider false.

- Complete the following table, according to the information given in the text:
  eg 'If you want to be successful in an interview, which of the following are
  a always important
  b sometimes important
  c occasionally important?'

	always	sometimes	occasionally
Dressing smartly Arriving early Knowing a lot about the company Appearing relaxed			

• Using the information in the texts, decide the following:

What should you do if you can't decide which subjects to study at university?

you are stuck in a traffic jam and know you'll be late for a job interview?

Where should you go if you want a cheap Chinese meal in Oxford?

you want to buy tickets for 'Phantom of the Opera'?

2 ■ Every student in the class is given the same text with three paragraphs or clearly defined sections. Each student silently reads the complete text. The class divides into three and each group reads a different paragraph in detail, looking up unknown words in dictionaries and/or discussing them with their groupmates and the teacher. Each group now prepares six questions about their particular paragraph to ask the two other groups of students. In preparing the questions, students should also make sure they note down the answers. New groups of three are then formed, with one representative from each of the previous groups in each. In turn, each student asks his questions to the other two, who will only have read the relevant paragraph in general at the start of the lesson. Students compete to find the necessary information as quickly as possible, with help from the questioner if necessary. When all the questions have been asked and answered, the groups can piece together all their information and discuss everything they know about the text.

3 The class is divided into two. Group A is given one practical, information-based text, eg 'How to apply for a driving licence' and group B is given another, eg 'How to apply to do an English course at a language school'. Each group then prepares questions about their text, such as 'Who should I send the form to?', 'How long will I have to wait?', 'How long are your courses?', 'Do I have to send a deposit?'. Pairs then form with one student from group A and one from group B. They exchange texts and read them through quickly to get the gist. They are now ready to perform a role-play. For example, student A now 'telephones' student B to inquire (using her list of questions) about how to apply for a driving licence. Student B, the

receptionist (who now has the information in front of him) looks for the answers and tries to help. Student B then 'telephones' A to enquire about English courses and A is now the receptionist who consults the information and responds.

4 The teacher gives everyone in the class a sheet of questions to be answered. The class is divided into three groups, with each group given a different short text describing specific aspects of the same person, place, event or experience. Students then read the information and, together with other members of their group, answer as many questions on the sheet as they can. Groups of three are now formed, with one student from each original group. The groups now work through the question sheet and find the information they don't know by asking each other – together they should have all the answers.

Guessing unknown words

1 The teacher writes some sentences on the board which include a difficult, probably unknown, word, but which give a good clue as to what the word might be.

eg: You look *grim*. Is anything wrong?
The curtains were *faded*. You couldn't see their original colours anymore.
The time *dragged*. I thought the meeting would never end.
There was an *uproar* when the election result was announced. We were all shocked.
One of the *hazards* of winter is black ice on the roads.

Students in pairs discuss

- **a** the type of word – adjective, noun, verb, etc – and the function it has in the sentence
- **b** whether the word has positive/negative/neutral effect
- **c** the context (writers often say the same thing twice, or give further information to reinforce their point. What does the rest of the context tell the reader which might help?)
- **d** what they think the word means in the context.

Class discussion follows.

2 Using English-English dictionaries, pairs of students find words that they think other students will not be familiar with. When they are themselves sure of the meaning and have discussed usage with the teacher, they incorporate these words into sentences of their own devising (as the teacher did in activity 1) and then pass them to other students to work out meanings.

3 All students are given the same text. The teacher writes a list of words and expressions on the board and asks them to find words in the text that mean the same. For example for a text which reads:

> Many people claim to have seen UFOs these days, although sceptics say that these are simply man-made objects flying around in the sky.

the teacher could write:

> Find a word in the text which means 'people who doubt something, or disbelieve it'.

Students could also create these kinds of questions for each other.

4 Each student is given the same text and asked to underline any words that she doesn't understand. After doing this students then form groups of four and ask each other about the words they have underlined. If another student knows the meaning of a word he explains it. Those words which no one knows, and which are considered important for the general meaning of the passage are then analysed and discussed. Concentration here should be on a), b), c) and d) on p27.

As a general rule, students should be encouraged to help each other with word meanings. When a student says, 'What does X mean?' the teacher should not answer until it is apparent that no one in the room has the answer except herself.

Inferential reading

1 All students read the same text and individually write down six things they know for *sure* from the text:

eg: The writer is a man.
James lives in the city centre.
Mrs Duncan has a dog called Foxy.
etc

They then compare their lists with a partner. If students have different items on their lists, they can then try to find the place in the text where their partner found the item they don't have.

2 Using the same text as in the activity above, students individually write down six things that they *imagine* to be true about the passage but are not told directly

eg: Paul's mother seems to be angry.
The writer seemed undecided about which route to take.
The writer seemed to be afraid of the people in the boat.
etc

Again, they compare lists in pairs and try to find where in the text their partner found the information that led him to deduce the above. Class discussion follows, with the teacher acting as arbiter.

3 ■ All students are given a narrative which includes one or more character portraits. In pairs, they write as much as they can infer about the feelings of the characters in the situations in the text. They then join up with another pair and discuss how they made their deductions, and whether there is sufficient evidence for them. This activity can be repeated with other kinds of text. For instance, with a text describing a place or building, students could be asked to infer atmosphere, while in a factual text students would note anything they feel the writer expects the reader to know about already or whether they feel he is for or against the topic he is writing about.

4 All students have the same text. They divide into groups of four. The teacher reads aloud a statement about the text, and each group decides if it is true or false. The statements must be about inferred information only – not about facts which are directly stated. For instance, 'The house is on a hill' may be implied in the text by a description of the 'magnificent view of the surrounding countryside below'. This activity can be turned into a game as described below on p36 – ie each group decides if the sentence is true or false. They win a point if they are correct, and lose one if they are wrong. Groups can then win further points by being the first to state where in the text they can find the information which proves or disproves the statement.

Extracting central ideas and summarising

1 All students are given the same information-based texts and the teacher writes four sentences on the board about each. For one text this could be:

eg: The leaflet is to

A tell you how to apply for a new passport
B give more information about the new-style passports
C be used as a passport if the original is lost
D explain the new immigration laws in the European Community

Students discuss in pairs which of the sentences best sums up the text and then report back to the class. Summarising statements for another passage might read: What was the writer's main reason for wanting to travel round the USA?

A to write a travel book
B to see towns he had not been to before
C to find out more about public transport
D to visit his relatives

2 Students are all given the same information – based on a factual text. In pairs they write a sentence saying what the passage is about, eg 'It's about Gatwick Airport',

followed by a maximum of three sentences summarising what each main idea expressed in the text is about:

eg:
- Gatwick is situated in the countryside but it is easily accessible from London.
- The airport there has created a lot of jobs for local people.
- Future developments will probably cause controversy in the surrounding area.

Two pairs join together to compare their summaries, discussing which is best and why. Class discussion follows.

3 Students work in pairs. Each pair is given a pack of short extracts from texts. Each pack consists of three whole texts cut up into parts, each part containing a maximum of two or three sentences. The students spread the extracts around a table and try to divide them into three piles, according to which text they belong to. They then discuss what seem to be the general idea behind each text, before arranging the extracts into a logical order. This done, they compare their order with that of another pair, and when they agree, the four students write a two or three sentence summary of the main ideas expressed in each of the texts. Finally, groups contribute to a class discussion, where each text is commented on, and the teacher writes each group's summary on the board for the class to decide which is best.

4 A final activity, another jigsaw reading idea which practises many of the skills required in Section B of paper 1, is as follows:

Students sit in circles (a maximum of twenty in each) and each person is given one sentence of a text of any kind at random. They then read aloud their sentences around the circle, after which they:

- discuss what the text is about
- discuss what they think the central ideas are
- move so that each student is sitting with other students whose sentences may have a similar theme and discuss any unknown words
- reorder themselves within their groups, according to link words in their extracts
- order themselves within the whole circle so that the text reads logically (see pp41–2)
- look at the whole text and answer, in pairs, questions about it which the teacher hands out or puts on the board after all the above stages have been completed
- discuss the correct answers to the questions.

Multiple-choice questions

1 The same text is given to all the students in the class. Students read the text. A set of answers to *one* multiple-choice question (which could be taken from a past examination paper) is given out and students in pairs work on finding the question:

eg: **A** People now live all over the country.
B Roads can take you to every corner of the country.
C There are maps of every corner of the country.
D People travel around more.

The question could then be 'Why are there so few unexplored places left in Britain?' This activity can now be expanded with further multiple-choice answers from the same text. Pairs then share their questions with the class. The teacher writes the questions on the board and class discussion follows as to which questions best fit the answers. If past papers are used in this way, students can then compare with the actual questions asked. The object in doing this is to give students practice 'reading' the examiners' minds and intentions, and making them familiar with the psychology of setting multiple-choice questions.

2 ■ The same text is given to each student. Students read the text. The class is divided into two. One group has five questions and must create multiple choice answers for each of them, only one of which is correct. The other group is given five sets of answers and must create the questions. Pairs then form, with one student from each group, and they discuss the questions and answers they have created with each other, and compare with the original if a past paper has been used.

3 All students are given the same set of five multiple-choice questions and answers, and individually think about the type of text that the questions are about. They discuss their ideas with their partner. Pairs then decide in more detail what the text is about – how much information about it they can find from the questions. Pairs then join together with another pair and pool all the information they have. Finally, students look at the original text and find out how close they were in their deductions.

4 All students read the same text and look at the set of five multiple-choice questions which follow it. In pairs they discuss:

- which of the distractors cannot be correct, and why
- which two distractors might be correct at first glance, and which information in the text eliminates them on closer inspection
- which answer must be correct and which information in the text acts as 'evidence' for it

Class discussion follows as pairs compare their findings. The teacher intervenes only at the last moment after the class has done as much work as possible independently.

5 ■ The class is divided into two groups. Students in group A are given text A to read, while group B students read text B. In pairs they then write five multiple-choice questions about the text, each one containing:

- an improbable answer
- two distractors which may be possible at first glance but on closer reading could not be
- a correct answer

Each group comes together to discuss which are the best multiple-choice questions from those pairs have written. When each group has decided, texts and questions are exchanged between groups who then work on answering each other's questions. Full class discussion takes place in the latter stages of the lesson.

6 ■ Every student in the class is given either a question or one multiple-choice answer, preferably from a past paper. An example is:

S1: Why does the writer say that 'there were few undiscovered corners of Britain'?
S2: Lots of people have seaside holidays.
S3: To get an idea for a book.
S4: Why did the author go by train?
S5: You meet interesting people on such a trip.

So if there are twenty students, four questions and sixteen multiple-choice answers will be used. The students' task is to sort out which answers fit which questions. They do this either by walking around the room and asking other people to read aloud the sentence they have, or by sitting in a circle and asking each other. Groups are formed of students whose questions and answers fit. When there are five clear groups (or three or four if there are fewer students), the class comes together and reports its questions and answers to the teacher who writes combinations on the board. Students now discuss the kind of text they think the questions and answers are about. Finally they see the text (and the questions if it is a past examination paper) and in pairs find the correct answer to each question. Pairs then report back to the teacher and the rest of the class. Where such movement around the classroom proves impossible, the component parts of the questions can be given on pieces of paper to pairs of students who then complete the activity as above.

CHAPTER 2

Paper 2
Composition

GENERAL DESCRIPTION

The Composition paper requires candidates to write two compositions of 120–180 words each from a choice of five titles. These fall into five clearly defined categories, which are described below.

As far as the marking system is concerned, the General Handbook goes into some detail which we summarise in this paragraph. When an impression assessment of each composition is made, a mark out of 20 is given, 8 – ie 40 per cent – being considered a rough pass. The Handbook sets out the factors that have to be taken into account in order to arrive at this mark, which may be summarised as follows: Each question provides a different task, therefore demanding different techniques and approaches. The examiner has to consider whether the task has been carried out in a relevant, organised way, using appropriate vocabulary, a range of lexical expressions, correct grammatical construction, and correct spelling and punctuation. A more detailed breakdown of the scales which form the basis for awarding the impression mark for each composition is as follows:

Marking
In the impression assessment given for each composition, a mark of about 40% of the total (i.e. 8 out of 20) is taken as a rough pass, and 75–90% a very good pass.

The following scales form the basis for awarding an impression mark for each composition.

18–20	Excellent	Natural English with minimal errors and complete realisation of the task set.
16–17	Very good	More than a collection of simple sentences, with good vocabulary and structures. Some non-basic errors.
12–15	Good	Simple but accurate realisation of the task set with sufficient naturalness of English and not many errors.
8–11	Pass	Reasonably correct but awkward and non-communicating OR fair and natural treatment of subject, with some serious errors.
5–7	Weak	Original vocabulary and grammar both inadequate to the subject.
0–4	Very poor	Incoherent. Errors show lack of basic knowledge of English.

Examiners attend a standardisation meeting to determine what exactly is meant by each of these guidelines. Also, at this meeting they mark a cross section of papers and discuss marks given according to the scales. As far as possible, then, the Board tries to ensure the inevitable subjectivity of the marking is as standardised and systematic as composition assessment allows.

DIFFERENT TYPES OF COMPOSITION

A letter

This can be personal or formal. Candidates are expected to set out the letter correctly with dates and addresses not included in the total number of words used. **a** below is an example of a personal letter, **b** demands more formal wording throughout:

a You have received an invitation to an engagement party, but it is impossible for you to accept it. Write a letter to your friend, explaining your reasons.

b Write a letter to a language school to enquire about a language course. Explain when you wish to attend and the type of course you would like.

Candidates are thus expected to have a sense of appropriacy with regard to language use, and an understanding of and control over the different styles in which people address each other.

A written speech

This can also be of a personal or formal nature – a personal speech requires candidates to imagine what they might say to a certain person in a given situation whereas a formal speech would be something that could be read aloud on a ceremonial occasion such as a wedding or retirement party. Two examples are:

a Explain, as if you were talking to a small child, how you learned to ride a bicycle.

b You are a famous personality invited to your old school to open a new shopping centre in the town you grew up in. What will you say in your speech?

A narrative or descriptive piece

Here students must write either a narrative telling a sequence of events in story form, or a description of a place, person or object. The narrative is often built around a dramatic phrase such as 'I knew I could never succeed' which could be given as either the first or last sentence of the story with candidates writing the rest. Examples of each kind of essay follow:

a It was the most exciting day of my life.
b Describe a journey on which you met a particularly interesting person.

Imagination, accuracy, organisational ability, conciseness, fluency – both language-specific and non-language-specific features are all called into play here.

Arguing a point

Candidates are requested to consider a statement and express their personal opinions. Examples are:

a Television does more harm than good? What is your opinion?
b Should policemen carry guns?

Once again, factors other than the purely linguistic operate here, for unless candidates have thought about the matter under debate in the question they cannot be expected to write a convincing composition.

Question on set books

In order to give themselves a fifth choice of title for this paper many candidates study a set book from a choice of three. This has advantages other than an extra choice of composition inasmuch as students can give themselves more security by reading a book they know they will be questioned on. Obviously, the types of questions depend on the book and its contents. Typically, a question chooses a character, event, quotation or thematic area and asks students to explain its significance in the book as a whole. Examples might be:

L P Hartley: 'The Go Between' – Do you think this is a good title? Explain the reason for your answer.
George Orwell: 'Animal Farm' – Who is Boxer and what part does he play in the book?

BREAKDOWN OF SKILLS NEEDED

From our review of the types of composition usually included in this paper, it is clear that students need:

- to write grammatically accurate individual sentences (relevant throughout the paper)
- to punctuate correctly (relevant throughout the paper)
- to end paragraphs and begin new ones at appropriate points in the composition (relevant throughout the paper)

- to write sentences that accurately connect with each other to form a text, ie link sentences with ones before and after in a cohesive manner (relevant throughout the paper)
- to adapt the style of English according to the degree of formality involved in the relationship between writer and reader (especially relevant to Questions 1 and 2)
- to manage certain everyday functions such as accepting and refusing invitations, making requests, giving advice, complaining, making inquiries, giving personal information, making suggestions (especially relevant to Question 1)
- to set out a letter according to accepted conventions, ie where to put the date, address, how to begin and end the letter appropriately (especially relevant to Question 1)
- to write a piece of extended narrative in the past tense, involving sequential ability to put one fact or event before another in a coherent manner (especially relevant to Questions 3 and 5)
- to write a piece of extended description of a scene, person or event, involving considerable control over vocabulary use (especially relevant to Questions 3 and 5)
- to express opinions and organise them into a format in which they may be readily understood by the reader, eg an 'advantages of . . .' paragraph followed by a 'disadvantages of . . .' paragraph. (especially relevant to Questions 4 and 5)

In addition to these linguistic factors, students will also need practice in how to make the right personal choice of two compositions from five.

SUGGESTED CLASSROOM ACTIVITIES

Writing grammatically accurate sentences

1 Students are divided into three, four or five teams. The teacher either says or writes on the board a sentence which may or may not be grammatically correct. In their teams the students must decide if the sentence is correct or incorrect. If they decide it is incorrect, they must then correct it. The teacher then asks one student from each team to give their decision and, where relevant, the correct version of the sentence. A point is awarded to each team for each correct decision, and two points for each correctly amended sentence where necessary. The process is repeated for the length of the lesson. This is an enjoyable way to revise basic structures already taught.

2 Students need practice with the word order of sentences. One way of doing this is to divide the class into groups of six or more students, ask each group to sit in a circle and give each student a card with a word written on it. If there are, say, eight students in the group and eight individual words, the words, put in the correct order, form a complete sentence. The students' task, then, is to decide the correct word order by saying their words and discussing how to reorder them. One student could write the correct version agreed on. After deciding, the cards are collected, and a further set of cards with different words distributed and the procedure repeated. An extension of this would be to include a set of words that do not quite make a complete sentence. The students then put their individual cards into an order as close as possible to a correct sentence, before discussing what is wrong with the sentence and how to make it correct. Obviously, the teacher monitors throughout, bringing the class together if necessary.

3 Students' written work is perhaps the best starting point for grammatical errors within sentences. In marking compositions the teacher could develop a marking code system, such as 'WO' for 'Word Order', 'T' for 'Tense', 'Sp' for 'Spelling', ⋌ for missing word, etc. Students are then encouraged to correct their own and/or others' written mistakes.

Punctuation

1 Students are given texts without punctuation and asked to work in pairs on supplying the full stops, commas, quotation marks, capital letters and other punctuation marks. Their own punctuated versions are compared with the originals, followed by discussion as to other possibilities.

2 Students find their own texts, depunctuate them and give them for their classmates to punctuate. Again, comparison with the original text follows.

Paragraphing

1 A good sensitisation to the necessity for paragraphing is a similar exercise to the punctuation exercise above where students have to paragraph an unparagraphed text.

2 Alternatively, a text could be rewritten, with paragraph breaks in odd and unexpected places. Students then paragraph correctly.

Writing sentences to form a text

This is an important and often neglected area called 'Cohesion'. Students need exercise-type practice in a systematic manner in order to write without repeating information unnecessarily. We go into it in some detail here. We suggest the exercises are done in the order given: in each case we provide two or three examples and leave the teacher to write further material along the lines indicated. It is important that the teacher draws students' attention to the level of formality of the connectors in the relevant exercises.

1 PRONOUN SUBSTITUTION

Students fill in the correct pronouns in the following paragraphs:

a Most of the old people who went on the trip to Brighton enjoyed............... However............... thought............... would have been better if the bus had left earlier so that...............had had longer...............

b More women than men learn foreign languages. Perhaps............... have more time or are simply better at...............

c Mike: Where are the books I left on the table?
Sally: Do you mean the............... with the torn covers?
Mike: No, not............... The............... in the brown paper.
Sally: Oh,............... Sorry, I've thrown............... away. I didn't think you wanted............... any more.
Mike: Oh no, Sally,............... are library books.

2 WORD FAMILY OR ALTERNATIVE NOUN SUBSTITUTION

Students find an alternative noun to substitute in these sentences:

a After breakfast I took leave of the others and turned my mind to the ascent of the peak. I did not think the............... looked too difficult.

b Elvis Presley died suddenly in August 1977. The............... was only 42 but had been in poor health for some time.

c Old Mrs Clark usually has a vase of tulips on her sideboard in springtime. She says spring wouldn't be the same without the...............

3 CREATING COHESION FROM NON-COHESION

The second sentence in the following short texts is artificial: it is not cohesive with the first. Students rewrite it to avoid repetition.

a I wish I could find the right advice to give you. There must be some advice I could give you but I don't know what advice I could give you.

b Jeremy won't be at Paul and Paula's wedding on Saturday week. Edward won't be at Paul and Paula's wedding on Saturday week either.

c Keith said he was going to a booking agency to buy a ticket for the England-Bulgaria match on the 23rd. Alan asked him if he could get him a ticket for the England-Bulgaria match on the 23rd, as he was going to the booking agency to buy a ticket for the England-Bulgaria match anyway.

4 CONNECTORS RELATED TO TIME

First; Before, Previously; Afterwards; Then; Next; Meanwhile; In the meantime; Finally; At last; Eventually
Choose from the above:

a Sir Hubert Morris is retiring next spring and going to live in Devon. ....he intends to continue working at the foreign office.

b I certainly hope everyone will think about the matters raised today very carefully. ...., I should like to thank all of you for attending.

c As soon as the Masons moved into their house, they started decorating. They couldn't stand the wallpaper left by the people who had lived there................

5 CONNECTORS MOVING FROM ONE SUBJECT OR IDEA TO ANOTHER

Speaking of / That reminds me / By the way / Incidentally / That brings me on to / As for / Anyway / Now for / Let us now turn to
Choose from the above:

a Ann can't come tomorrow – she's working late. ...., have you claimed your overtime for last month?
b There can be little doubt, then, that striptease clubs serve a useful purpose in the community. .... my next subject – prostitution.
c Sorry, I can't come to Greece at Easter after all. I've got an essay to write and ought to visit my mother. ...., I can't afford it.

6 CONNECTORS GIVING A CONTRAST OR OPPOSITE

Instead / On the contrary / In fact / However / But / Nevertheless / All the same / On the one/other hand
Choose from the above:

a Women are superior drivers to men in every respect – they are safer and more polite. ...., men are better cyclists.
b I didn't ask her to leave. ...., I asked her to stay.
c My attitude towards television is ambivalent. ...., I think it does a lot of good, as it provides pleasure and company for old people. ...., I am less happy about the effect on children of some of the more violent programmes.

7 CONNECTORS GIVING A RESULT

So / Therefore / Hence / Thus / As a result
Choose from the above:

a Late night Monday shopping in the department stores has run at a considerable loss. ...., we propose to close all our branches at 6.00 pm on Mondays as from the beginning of next month.

b When Jack was in Italy last year he ran out of money. .... he had to come home.

8 CONNECTORS ADDING INFORMATION OR REINFORCING A POINT

Also / And another thing / Moreover / Furthermore / In fact / Indeed / In other words / After all / I mean . . .
Choose from the above:

a I'm sick of the way you keep slamming the door when you come home at night. ...., could you ask before you borrow the toothpaste?

b There is often a thin line between fact and fiction. ...., I often wonder if there is any difference at all between them.

c Attitudes to Christmas seem to get more hypocritical each year. ...., last night I had carol singers at the door and it's only November 11th.

9 CONNECTORS REFERRING FORWARD

My argument is as follows / As we shall see later / Here is why / Firstly
No discriminatory exercises are necessary here.

10 ■ SUPPLYING AN APPROPRIATE CONNECTOR

These two sentences are not cohesive. Supply an appropriate connector at the beginning of the second sentence to make it cohesive with the first choosing from any of the above connectors:

a Management has turned down the union's proposal for further pay negotiations. .... it has been decided to take industrial action as from Monday next.

b No good can be achieved by taking industrial action. .... a lot of harm will be done.

c There has been a general increase in slackness among the staff with several teachers being late for lessons and not marking homework properly. ...., you're all getting lazy!

d Between 1986 and 1987 Liz worked in an insurance office. .... she was at Queen Mary School, Hastings.

e Robert looked all over the house for his glasses – under cushions, all round the garden, in the attic, he even stripped his bed. ...., he found them in the garage inside his tool bag.

11 ■ WRITING A FIRST COHESIVELY ACCURATE SENTENCE WHEN THE SECOND IS GIVEN

In these examples the second sentence is given with a connector at the head of it. Write the first sentence.

a .... So we'd better stop.
b .... However, after discussions with management, we have decided against it.
c .... Anyway, I'm still going.
d .... Therefore the meeting has been postponed until a later date.
e .... I mean, why can't he bring his own car?

12 ■ WRITING A SECOND COHESIVELY APPROPRIATE SENTENCE WHEN THE FIRST IS GIVEN

Here are three first sentences. For each one write three second sentences beginning with the connectors given. They must be appropriate in meaning and level of formality:

a London bus drivers are to proceed with their one day strike next Monday.
1 However . . .
2 Meanwhile . . .
3 As a result . . .

b The number of accidents in the home increases each year.
1 Therefore . . .
2 In fact . . .
3 However . . .

c Oh, and I also went to the cinema with Peter yesterday.
1 By the way . . .
2 Anyway . . .
3 In fact . . .

13 PARAGRAPH JIGSAW

The 12 excercise outlines suggested above practise cohesion awareness between two sentences. Students can be sensitised to cohesion in a paragraph by putting a jumbled text into its correct order. They do this by dividing into groups and sitting in a circle. If there are eight students in each group, each student is given a sentence from a text. The students' task is to put the text into its correct order of eight sentences. They do this by saying their individual sentences, learning them and then putting them aside so that all the ordering work can be done orally. Dialogues too may be reordered in this way. (See p75) The more students and sentences, the more challenging the task. Here is an example of a simple eight-sentence text in diagrammatic form, with eight students in a circle:

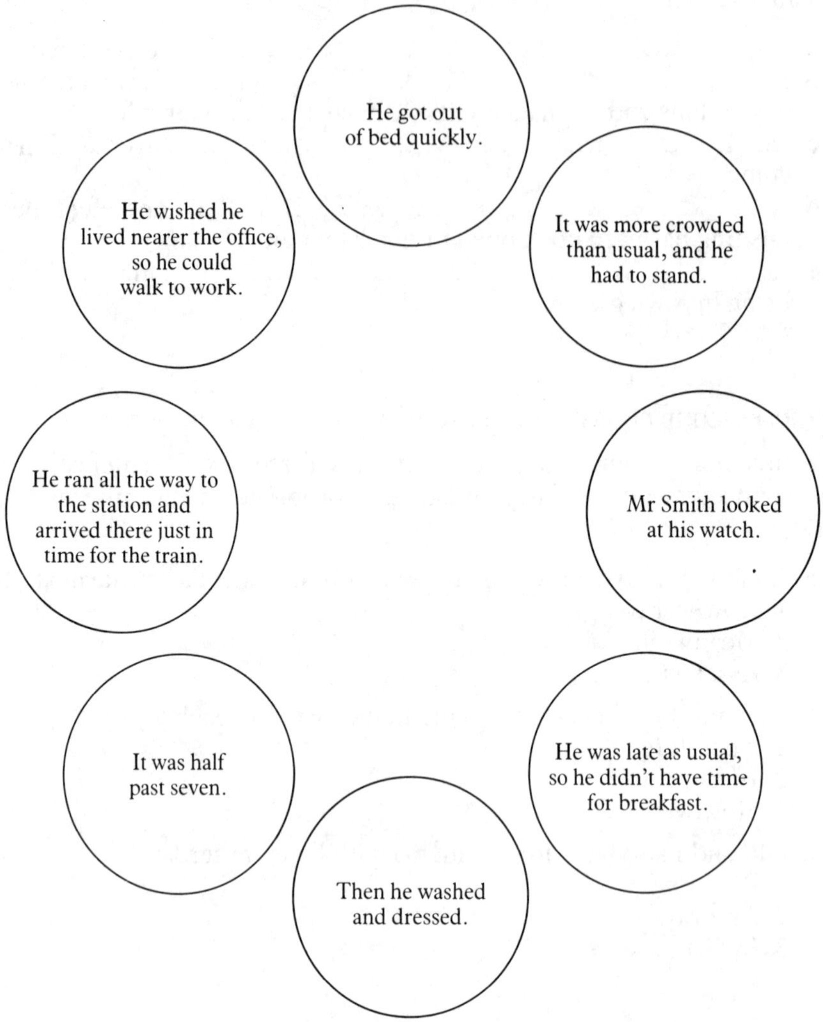

A variation on this idea is to omit two or three sentences. Students then not only have to decide the order of the text, but must work out, from the textual clues available, what is written in the missing sentences.

14 TEXT JIGSAW

Extending the idea above, students could be given individual paragraphs and asked to put them in order to make a complete text. Thus as on pp36–7 students created a sentence from words, and as on pp41–2 they created a paragraph from sentences, and here they create a text from paragraphs.

15 ■ PICTURE JIGSAW – WRITING A COHESIVE COMPOSITION FROM PICTURES

The teacher could take the following picture story and cut it up into 12 pieces:

Ideally, with this particular picture story there would be 12 students in the class. The students sit in a circle and the teacher gives each student one of the pictures. Each student orally describes his picture to the others, using the past tense. The teacher monitors and corrects. The students then decide on the correct order of the pictures for a sequential narrative. When they are agreed, the pictures are redistributed, and each student writes a grammatically correct sentence in the past tense for his new picture. The teacher writes each of the sentences on the board. A version of the picture story given here might be:

1 Last Sunday Bob and Ann drove to London Airport in a lot of traffic.
2 Bob and Ann were late at the airport and had to check in their luggage.
3 They ran across the airport to catch their aeroplane.
4 Everyone was sitting in the aeroplane happily reading or sleeping.
5 The stewardess was taking refreshments to the passengers.
6 The wing of the aeroplane suddenly caught fire.
7 The stewardess went into the pilot's cabin to tell the pilot.
8 The stewardess went back and told the passengers to stay calm.
9 Bob and Ann and the passengers were very worried and afraid.
10 Air traffic control called the ambulance and fire brigade.
11 The aeroplane landed safely at the airport.
12 All the passengers were relieved to get off the aeroplane.

The students must now turn these 12 individual sentences into a cohesive text. For example, 'Bob and Ann' and 'airport' are repeated in sentence 2 and need to be replaced by pronouns. Information is also omitted – there are time 'jumps', for example, between pictures 2 and 3,3 and 4 and 10 and 11. Although the story might benefit from joining one or two sentences together, with more detailed description and some short conversational exchanges, the priority for the students here is to make it acceptable from a cohesion point of view.

16 ■ COMPLETING A TEXT FROM COHESIVE CLUES

Students are given incomplete texts and asked to complete them from the contextual clues. Beginning and ending sentences of paragraphs are particularly useful, as they make the students pay attention to what has gone before and what comes after, when thinking of what to write in between. Here is an example:

> When I was a child my parents usually took me to the seaside. As far as I remember, the sun shone every day. ....
> ....
> ....
>
> Not surprisingly, then, I was always sad when the holiday was over and we had to go back to the city. Now that I am an adult, the type of holiday I usually take has changed in some ways but not in others. ....
> ....
> ....

The trouble is, a day after I'm back at work again, I've forgotten all about it. Of course, everyone has their own idea of a perfect holiday, and I'm no exception. ....
....
....
Still, I can dream, can't I?

17 BUILDING A CLASS COMPOSITION FROM SEPARATE PIECES OF INFORMATION

Each student is given a card. On each card is the name of a building in a town called Heathwick. There are six different buildings, so two people in a class of 12 are given, unknown to each other, the same building on a piece of card. Each student is then asked to write one sentence about his building. The 12 sentences are brought together and written on the board before the class works, in groups of two, three or four, on putting the 12 sentences about the six buildings into a piece of continuous writing called 'Guidebook Description of Heathwick', paying particular attention to the cohesive links. Contradictory information has to be sorted out and an introductory paragraph written. If the class is larger (or smaller), the number of cards is amended accordingly. Here are the 12 sentences one class wrote (after grammatical mistakes had been corrected):

Police Station

1 The police station was built in the mid-70s and stands in the centre of the shopping centre opposite the library.

2 The police station is modern and square-shaped and was built by a local architect.

Library

1 The library is ten years old and specialises in children's literature.

2 The library, a large red-brick building, was built ninety years ago.

The Yellow Submarine

1 In the middle of the town there is a pub with a lot of charm and character.

2 The pub is in the old part of the town and serves food at lunchtimes.

The George Hotel

1 The George is in the middle of the town: it is a four-star hotel and is owned by the Crawford family.

2 The George is the main hotel with a large car park.

St Mary's Church

1 The oldest building in Heathwick is the church which was built in the fourteenth century.

2 St Mary's Church which stands in London Road was built in the nineteenth century.

Other suggestions for this kind of treatment are: 'General Description of a Market on a Saturday morning'. Two cards for each of the following; food stalls; antique stalls; secondhand clothes stalls; the pub at lunchtime; people in the crowd. 'Description of your bedroom in a letter to a friend'. Two cards for: the bed; the chairs; the table; the curtains; the ornaments; the carpet; the wallpaper; the general atmosphere

Adapting style to the degree of formality

1 A sensitisation exercise of the type below can be set. Students are informed that although the grammer is correct in every case, the sentences are not suitable for the contexts in which they occur. Their task is to say where each would be more appropriate, and what would be better suited to the particular situation given here.

What people say	**Example of situation for which it would be appropriate**	**The English more suited to the situation**
I should be pleased to invite you to my birthday party (letter to a close friend)		
I want another piece of apple pie (said to a landlady)		
Perhaps you would be so kind as to telephone me soon (to a close friend)		
Susan always has such a sense of animation about her (spoken to a close friend)		
Stop being so fussy (said to someone not met before at a dinner party)		
Further to our telephone conversation I write to confirm (after a phone call to a good friend)		

2 Students could be given extracts from different letters like those below. Their task is to decide if each should come at the beginning, middle or end of the letter and grade them according to levels of formality – from extremely formal, to casual:

- **a** I look forward to hearing from you as soon as possible
- **b** I'm sorry I haven't written for so long. What with one thing and another I just haven't had the time.
- **c** Anyway, must dash or I'll miss the post.
- **d** I've been here a month now and I'm beginning to get used to it.
- **e** Enclosed is my remittance for £20, this being the payment for . . .
- **f** I must therefore inform you that unless I receive satisfaction within three days . . .
- **g** Time has flown and I can't believe I've only got three more days to go.
- **h** Thank you so much for inviting me to your party of 10th May.
- **i** He expects to arrive at 7.00 pm on 3rd September and would like dinner.
- **j** Do you think you could come and meet me? I've got so much luggage.

3 ■ Each student could be set the task of finding three letters in newspapers and magazines if these are available – one very personal and chatty, the second fairly neutral and the third formal. Problem page letters are useful for personal styles, letters to the editor can be personal or neutral, especially in local newspapers and the popular press, and examples of formal style may be found in letters to quality newspapers. Students pool their letters in groups, discuss styles and contents, then choose one of the letters to answer in the style in which it was written (or, if they choose, a deliberately different style). This is a sophisticated activity and may be hard going with a weak class.

4 ■ Students could be given practice in transferring the Latinisms which many Europeans prefer to their phrasal verb equivalents which most English speakers use in both speaking and writing. Dictionaries might be useful here. This is a possible exercise:

- **a** Andrew couldn't *tolerate* the situation a moment longer.
- **b** You didn't believe him, did you? Almost everything he says is *fabricated*.
- **c** The motion will be *submitted* for discussion at the next meeting.
- **d** She's always *chastising* me for being so untidy.
- **e** The reviews *dissuaded* me *from* seeing the film.
- **f** The good food more than *compensated* for the bad service.
- **g** I don't really want to go to the meeting, but how can I *extricate myself*?
- **h** She hasn't a good word to say for him: she's always *belittling* him.

Similar exercises could be set for noun and adjective practice.

5 Awareness of formality is particularly important in the letter composition. One of the best ways of sensitising students in this area is to set them a short letter writing task, then write a cross-section of what they have written on the board and discuss in class which language is too formal and informal for the situation, and which totally appropriate. For example, students could be set the following task:

> You've decided to have a party on Saturday 22nd November. Write a letter to a close friend inviting her/him to the party. Use no more than 20 words.
> In the letter **a** tell your friend about the party
> **b** invite him/her
> **c** end appropriately

While students are writing, the teacher goes around the class, noting down who is writing what. The 'telling about the party' section might include 'I write to invite you', 'I have a birthday party', 'I should be pleased to announce my birthday party', 'I'm having a party on 22nd November' or 'I celebrate my birthday with a little party'. When the teacher has a number of varied openings, she can write them on the board. Students first correct the grammar, then, in pairs, put the sentences into levels of formality. The sentences they have written are usually much too formal for the occasion, and at their worst may be on the lines of 'I should be honoured if you would kindly accept this invitation'. Students are often surprised to find a good letter consists of nothing more than

> 'I'm having a party on Saturday 22nd November. Can you come? Give me a ring and let me know, will you? Love . . .'

As a follow-up students write letters accepting and refusing the invitation as informally and in as few words as possible.

6 A similar personal letter written in too formal a style is given to students who then rewrite it in suitably informal English. Perhaps individual students could do this at home, then in class 'share' what they have written with their classmates. Much discussion about language will ensue.

7 A similar exercise can be done in reverse, ie a business letter written in a personal, chatty tone could be rewritten in an appropriately detached, formal English.

8 Students should be encouraged to write to each other. As they are classmates, the style is likely to be informal/personal. For example, if a student has a suggestion for a weekend activity he wishes to make to another student, he writes it in a letter and delivers it instead of saying it. The recipient then writes a letter in reply. If a student is absent or unwell, the class can write a joint letter and send it, paying attention not just to correctness of structure but also appropriacy of style. Many other student-student, student-teacher letters will occur spontaneously once students have got into the habit.

9 Letter conventions also need to be taught – date, address, lay-out, manner of address and endings. After this has taken place, students spend five or ten minutes putting the right ending with the right beginning, according to level of formality. Here is an example:

Dear Sir	With kind regards
Dear Mary (your sister)	Yours sincerely
Dear Mrs Jones (a customer)	Love
Dear Dad	Best Wishes
Dear Mrs Jones (ex-landlady)	Cheers
Dear Paul (a friend)	Yours faithfully
Dear Doctor Stephens	See you soon

As there is no exact one-to-one correspondence, there is much for pairs and small groups to discuss here.

Managing everyday functions

1 During their course students need to revise basic functional English like that mentioned in the 'Breakdown of skills' section. This language should not be new to them at this level, and there is, in fact, little difference between spoken and written styles, particularly in the kinds of letters they are asked to write in this paper. One way of emphasising this would be to take some past composition titles and practise them first as telephone conversations.

A typical example would be:

> 'You have won a holiday for two in New York. Write to a friend describing the holiday, and inviting him or her to go with you.'

Students are asked to role-play, in pairs or with the teacher, the phone conversation that might take place. Three or four different paired conversations could be recorded and played back to the students with class correction and discussion. A correct and appropriate conversation is then written on the board which students copy and, for homework, turn the phone call into the letter demanded by the examination. Most other Question 1 letters lend themselves to this kind of treatment.

2 A composition based on the examination paper can be set for students with the functions outlined – students must provide the actual English.

An example might be:

> 'A friend of yours is coming to work in your town. Write to him or her giving some information, and suggesting where to stay and what to do in the first few weeks.'

and could look like this:

Dear Karen,

First Paragraph	1 Thank her for her letter and acknowledge receiving the information that she is coming to work in your town 2 Express pleasure at this news
Second Paragraph	3 Give information about the town – geographical situation, entertainment facilities, places of interest, etc.
Third Paragraph	4 Make a suggestion about accommodation for the first few weeks. Give reasons and information, 5 Make an alternative suggestion with advantages and possible drawbacks. 6 End the letter suitably.

Students could work in pairs on each of the above systematically, with the teacher bringing them together as a class after each has been written to discuss accuracy and levels of formality.

3 The class could be divided into two groups. Two letter assignments are set – a different one for each group. Each group divides into pairs who then write their own letter. The group comes together, passes round the letters the pairs have written and appoints a scribe who writes the perfect composite group letter which is then given to the other group to reply to. When the replies have been written, they are exchanged and discussed.

Setting out a letter

1 After the letter conventions have been taught, students could be asked to correct an incorrectly set-out letter

eg:

thomas jones
22nd April — king street 50 London
kensington

dear andy

many thanks for your letter...

....

....

faithfully yours

Thomas

2 The activities suggested on pp76–8 are also relevant to letter writing.

Writing extended narrative in the past tense

1 Although it is assumed that students preparing for the FCE have learned regular and irregular past tense forms, further practice may be necessary. A gap-fill where the correct verb must first be chosen, then put into its past tense form could prove useful. The one below is an example:

Put the 34 missing verbs in their correct past form in the following spaces:

> Mary's Weekend
>
> Last Friday at 5 pm Mary (1)............... work and (2)............... to the supermarket. When she (3)............... home she (4)............... a meal for herself, (5)............... a comedy programme on TV, (6)............... a bath and (7)............... to bed early, because she (8)............... tired.
>
> On Saturday morning she (9)............... down to Brighton to see her friends, David and Carol. It (10)............... a beautiful day so they (11)............... on the beach in the afternoon and (12)...............under the hot sun. In the evening they (13)............... David's brother, Jim, and (14)............... tennis. Mary (15)............... good-bye to her friends at 10 pm, (16)............... into her car and (17)............... back to London.
>
> Mary (18)............... up late on Sunday morning. She (19)............... in bed for some time and (20)............... the paper. At 11 am the phone (21)............... It (22)............... her boyfriend, Steve, who (23)............... her to meet him for lunch. The pub garden where they (24)............... was very crowded, so they (25)............... for a walk in Regent's Park and (26)............... the ducks on the lake. In the evening they (27)............... a good film in the cinema – "Rocky 55" – it (28)............... very funny and they (29)............... a lot. Afterwards they (30)............... a Chinese takeaway (31)............... it back to Steve's flat, (32)............... some coffee and (33)............... asleep around midnight. Mary (34)............... her weekend very much.

2 A Question 3 composition from a past paper can be set as a class composition. The teacher at the centre guides and monitors as students write in carefully controlled stages. The importance of this type of lesson is that it is the students' ideas which form the content of the composition. For example, let us assume this question has been set:

> 'A small boy runs away from his school after an argument. Describe what happened to him from the moment he left to the moment he was found again.'

On the board the teacher writes: 'How old was the boy?'
Students discuss in pairs, give suggestions to the teacher who writes up, eg: 'The boy was 9 years old'. Next the teacher writes 'What was his name?' Students discuss in pairs. Questions such as 'What was the argument about?', 'Who did he argue

with?' then follow. The board will now look something like this: 'The boy was 9. His name was Jimmy. He argued with his teacher. He arrived late for class.'

The sentences are short and disconnected, and the teacher asks students working in pairs to expand into one connected sentence, adding any information they think necessary. A connected sentence on the board at the end of pair discussion would be:

'Jimmy, a 9-year-old boy, arrived late for class; his teacher was angry and his mother was furious.'

The lesson format continues with students answering such teacher-controlled questions as: 'Where did he go? Why did he go there?' 'How did he feel?' 'Did he talk to anyone?', 'How did his parents feel when they realised he was gone?', 'How did they find out?', 'Did they phone the police?', 'Where was Jimmy found, and what was he doing at the time?', 'How did he get taken back to school?', 'Was everything all right in the end?' Students write a complete and more-or-less correct version for homework.

3 Students should be encouraged to write diaries on a regular basis. The more practice they have, writing about what they did yesterday or at the weekend, the more confident they will become at manipulating past tense forms in written narrative, as well as developing qualities such as self-awareness and imagination. Some students like keeping a diary and all should be allowed to choose whether or not to share this with the teacher and/or other students, or to keep it to themselves.

4 Picture compositions such as that on p43 are extremely useful in practising past tense narrative. The lesson outlined in this activity shows how past tenses can be built up by reordering the story. This time the group can take it further, building on the basic story line by repeating and elaborating adding information where necessary and inserting pieces of dialogue where they might add to the drama before finally writing a full-length version of the story, either in pairs in class, or individually for homework. Picture stories which have more than one possible chronological ordering are even more useful, as students may discuss and decide which of two or three possible sequences of pictures is the best.

5 Another way of dealing with picture compositions is to divide the class into pairs. One student, A, is given a complete picture story to tell in the past tense to his partner, B, who does not see the picture. If he doesn't understand, B may seek clarification from A. When this phase has finished, the teacher brings the class together and asks the B students to tell the story to her, one after the other, round the class. The A students correct if the information is incorrect, and the whole class comments on how interesting the story was. Usually, the story lacks drama and fluency, a fact which the class recognises. Students then may wish to add to the basic story line. The teacher can then explain he wishes the students to look at the story in more detail and can proceed in one of the following ways:

6 He can give the complete picture to the B students and ask different pairs to write about different pictures in as much detail as possible. So one pair writes about the first picture, another pair about the second, and so on. During this written phase the teacher goes around the class monitoring, correcting and supplying vocabulary where necessary. Finally, the class comes together as each pair shares the reading of what they have written. For homework each student writes a complete version of the story in the past tense, creating dialogue and dramatic interest wherever appropriate.

7 Alternatively, the teacher provides a controlled framework on the board – students must supply correct grammar and vocabulary in between. For example, if the material for the composition were the picture story on p43–4 the teacher might write:

> Last July Ann and George Lewis were catching a plane to Majorca at 12.00 pm. They .... 7.00 am but .... London Airport...................................
> .... traffic jam. They felt very.................. and ....

Pairs then write full versions. The teacher goes around monitoring before bringing the class together for suggested completions, asking a particular student either to complete on the board or read out what he has written for the teacher to write up. Class discussion follows before a fully correct board version is written. It may be advisable here to ask students to use two pieces of paper, one for the 'rough' version, the other for the correct one. The format is repeated until the lesson or picture story ends, and the complete narrative is written for homework. The advantage of this method is the amount of detail generated, forced into the composition, as it were, by the teacher's controlled structuring.

8 A looser way of treating a picture composition would be to give only certain vocabulary predicted by the story line. The task of the students is to use the words and phrases given in accurate and connected sentences. Staying with the 'airport/fire' story, the following vocabulary items might be written on the board or printed on paper. If verbs are supplied they are presented in their infinitive forms:

> traffic jam / check-in luggage / take off / relieved / wing on fire / cockpit / to reassure

Students build a sentence round each of the above and write the full story for homework.

9 Students may be asked to think of any of the following personal experiences:

> The first time I fell in love / smoked a cigarette / went abroad / took an examination / etc
> My most embarrassing moment / A time I lost something / My best/worst holiday / My first day at school / A film/book I particularly liked/disliked

or any subject which demands narrative in the past tense. Students form pairs and sit facing each other. Each pair decides who is student A, who student B. Student A is then given two or three minutes to tell student B her story in the past tense. Student B listens or keeps verbal interventions to the minimum so as not to detract from A's story. After the three minutes B tells A's story back to her in the first person as if it happened to him. A listens, then afterwards discusses how well she thought B had listened. The procedure is repeated with the roles reversed. Immediately afterwards, student A writes the story student B told her, student B writes student A's story – preferably still in the 1st person and supplying as much detail as possible. The stories are then exchanged, corrected and discussed.

10 Biographical pieces are useful for practising the past tense. Stage by stage, in class, students can be asked to expand notes into connected English. The teacher goes over each stage after students have written complete sentences individually or in pairs. Here is an example of material which could be used in this way:

The Life of Helen Winter

a Past Tense Reinforcement.
b Prepositions and Connectors.

Make sentences from the following notes:

paragraph one

1st sentence: 6 Vancouver, Canada February 22nd 1950

2nd sentence: father: engineer – mother: teacher

3rd sentence: youngest child – 3 older sisters

paragraph two

1st sentence: 1955–61 East Vancouver Primary School

2nd sentence: 1961–68 Vancouver Girl's High School – pass exams, including Economics and Mathematics with distinction.

paragraph three

1st sentence: 1968–74 Study Law at University of Ottawa.

2nd sentence: Degree in Law obtained. 1975 Move to London, England – work at firm of solicitors.

3rd sentence: 1976 Marry BBC

television journalist, David Porter. 1977 Birth of daughter, Marian.

4th sentence: 1978 Family move to Birmingham – husband's promotion. 1979 Birth of son, Clive.

5th sentence: 1980 Publication of first book, 'Women And The Law'. 1981 Start firm of legal advice with friend, Carol Colman.

paragraph four

Arrange the sentences

1983: Divorce from husband. Move back to London – found flat and lived with two children. 1984 – Arrest at Greenham Common for protesting against U.S. Nuclear Missiles. 1988 – Start writing weekly articles on 'Women And The Law' in magazine, 'Boadicea'.

11 Chain stories are useful. This is where one student begins a story in the past tense, the next continues where he left off, followed by the third student, and so on round the class. Any incorrect past tenses are corrected by the teacher, the students or the speaker himself.

Writing extended description

1 See pp45–6.

2 After the vocabulary of clothing and physical appearance have been taught, students could be put into pairs and given cards of people, preferably full-length and drawn in colour. Each pair has the same person with four or five small differences. Their task is to find these differences by orally describing the person in their pictures and the clothes they are wearing. The language used would probably consist of the following:

S1: She's wearing a red blouse
S2: Yes, so is mine. She's got a bracelet on her left wrist.
S1: Oh, mine hasn't.
S2: One difference then.

Such an 'Information Gap' activity gives students practice in using the vocabulary of physical description.

3 An extension of this is that each student is given a picture of a person as above, preferably full-length and drawn rather than photographed, and, working in a pair with another student, describes her person to her partner who draws the person from the description she hears. Comparison is then made with the original before the roles are reversed. Written description of the life of the person on the student's card follows. If difficulties arise, the teacher can prompt with questions such as:

Where does the person live? / What does he/she do for a living? / Family details? / Hobbies? / Where does he/she go on holiday? / What are the person's good and bad qualities? / etc

Even more challenging is for pairs to describe both people as occupants of the same railway carriage or sharing the same office – how would they get on together? If they met as a result of Computer Dating, how would this be? Imaginative students will come up with other ideas.

4 A good 'Information Gap' activity to describe places is for students, working in pairs, to each be given the same map of a town and the same names of buildings in that town written on small pieces of card. With a book as a barrier between them, student A places the cards on her map and then describes to student B the location of the places. Student B's task is to place her cards in exactly the same places on her map as A. On finishing the two students look at each other's map and discuss discrepancies before changing roles. Together, at the end, they decide on the best position for the building, draw this, give their town a name and, for homework, write a description for a tourist brochure, adding anything they think has been omitted.

5 Much the same kinds of activity as those described above can be applied to a description of a room – furniture and its arrangements instead of clothes and buildings.

6 Students together are asked to design either the perfect classroom or school building or town. This could begin at small group level – threes or fours – with discussions as to what aspects they would like to keep the same, and what changes they would wish to make. Delegates from each group move to other groups to explain their plans. Discussion between groups, and the whole class together then follows before pairs, groups or individuals write a composition entitled 'My Perfect Christmas/School/Town'.

7 Description of personality is an extremely complex and sophisticated area of English, and it is unlikely that at FCE level students will be expected to handle its nuances and subtleties. However, a few compositions expect students to have some ability to describe what people can do to make you feel a certain way about them

eg: 'Describe a journey on which you met a particularly interesting person'.

A lesson or lessons on, say, three things people do which you most like or dislike might prove useful. Individuals could do this for homework and share their writing with a partner, group or class. The teacher corrects the English and the students respond according to their own feelings. But generally speaking, the language of personality, relationships and emotions is above the level of First Certificate. See pp95–7 which give further help.

Expressing opinions and organising them into a composition

1 Many FCE compositions in Question 4 lend themselves to an 'Advantages and Disadvantages' type written format, or variations on it. An overall framework for such compositions is:

1st paragraph: the advantages	One of the best things about X is .... Another good thing is .... Thirdly, ...
2nd paragraph: the dis-advantages	On the other hand, there are a number of disadvantages. Firstly, ... In addition to this, ... Another drawback is .... Last but not least, ...
Brief summing up	On the whole, ...

Students can be given the above general framework and told that for homework they will be expected to write a composition based on it. Meanwhile, they will be divided into groups – one to think of the advantages of a particular topic, the other the disadvantages. This example of a composition title:

'Should policemen carry guns? Discuss.'

lends itself to this treatment, with Group A thinking of all the reasons why they shouldn't and Group B thinking of reasons why policemen should carry guns. A chairperson is appointed in each group to list the points the group has come up with. When the teacher brings the class together she lists the reasons for and against on the board, correcting and rewording where necessary. Students then practise orally 'fitting' their points into the format given, providing follow-up explanations for their points in each case, before writing the full composition for homework.

Even more apparently complicated titles lend themselves to this approach. For example:

'Television does more harm than good. What is your opinion?'

The formula presented above would need amending from 'One of the best things . . .' to 'One point in favour of the statement is . . .', 'Another reason why TV is harmful is . . .' but the basic idea is similar, as is the classroom process of groups for and groups against.

2 The best way to prepare students for written compositions giving opinions is probably through oral discussion work generally. This should develop students' abilities to think through and express their own opinions in English and to listen and respond to others'. Written composition at home could regularly follow class discussion, with students helping to correct each other's work following the teacher's marking code. Common themes for discussion include:

> Sport / Animal Welfare / Work and Leisure / Drink and Drugs / Smoking / Marriage and Family / Health and Fitness / Environment and Conservation / Music / Holidays / Education

indeed many of the themes covered by course books generally. Although in our experience the best discussions are likely to occur spontaneously, there is a necessity in the FCE classroom for the discussion lesson to be as institutionalised as any of the written skills lessons. If the classroom approaches suggested in this book are implemented, students will receive much practice in giving their opinions in the process of preparing for written work. See p57 for further guidance.

3 ■ Each student receives a card with a controversial opinion on it. She has 10 minutes to make notes before giving a two minute speech on the topic, which forces her either to agree or disagree with the argument. This could be turned into a team game with the other team awarding points out of ten for the speech, according to how accurate, fluent, well-organised and interesting they found it. The student then writes a paragraph or full composition for homework on the topic she talked on. Examples of topics are:

> All smokers are sick / Travel does not broaden the mind / No dogs should be allowed in cities / English is the world's most beautiful language / Women are better drivers than men / Television is the opium of the people

Topics should be adapted to the students' own cultural context and social interests. As this is quite a sophisticated exercise, teachers should not attempt it until students have had a variety of other types of oral practice and have grown in self-confidence.

4 Role-plays of committee meetings discussing such topics as

> Whether or not a local disco should be closed / Where a new road widening scheme should be developed in the town

are very good preparation for argument and opinion language. These can be recorded and played back and the language discussed and corrected by students and teacher. If the school or college has a video it can be put to excellent use here by video-recording proceedings as if for a TV magazine programme.

If for example, the disco theme is taken, different students take different roles – teenagers who go to the disco and like it, teenagers who have had bad experiences there, two groups of parents – those opposed, those in favour, neighbours who can't sleep, neighbours who can, police officers, disco managers, and a dj at the disco. Two students act as interviewers who control the whole proceedings, deciding on order of presentation, when to throw the debate 'open to the floor', how to co-ordinate, open and close. For homework, students stay 'in role', and write their arguments for or against. The students who had been chairpersons could write a composition weighing up the 'fors' and 'againsts' as shown on p57.

5 ■ More formal debates operate along similar lines. A possible subject would be:

'We believe capital punishment should be restored for terrorist attacks.'

Two students argue in favour, two against, with the chairperson then inviting comments and opinions from 'the floor' (the other students). Finally, a vote is taken, and the proposal passed or rejected. However, this activity may be well above the language abilities of many FCE candidates.

6 A variation of **3** above is for a group to sit in a circle and 'share' the subject under discussion. For instance if the topic is 'No one should be allowed to get married until they are 25', student A starts and when he has dried up, student B takes over, using phrases such as 'As A said . . .', 'Although I agree with what has been said, I also think . . .', 'Another point against/in favour . . .', 'On the other hand . . .'. This is a good way of ensuring everyone says something, and makes a subject a group event rather than an individual talk as in **3** above. Written homework could follow once students are familiar with points for and against as practised in the class exercise.

Choosing the right composition

Although in theory candidates have a choice of five compositions from which they must choose two, in effect the total is reduced to four if they have elected not to take the set book option. Whatever the situation, the matter of which compositions they choose may make all the difference between passing and failing. Making the right choice thus becomes crucial.

1 Students look at a selection of old papers and decide which two compositions they would choose to answer. They move into groups of four and discuss their choices, giving their reasons for doing so. The chairperson makes a list of the titles chosen, then when the class comes together, reports to the teacher and the rest of the students. The teacher makes a list of choices and numbers on the board. Often one composition is more or less ignored with one or two 'over-subscribed'. Class discussion follows. Generally speaking, it seems students choose question 1 and either question 2 or 3, believing question 4 to be more 'difficult'. Students can then take the question they like least to write at home or in class.

2 As a follow-on and, after a number of real and artificial papers have been reviewed, students, working in pairs, write four questions of the type normally occurring in the composition papers. In a class of sixteen, two groups of eight then form to role-play an examination committee moderating questions. The task is to choose four questions from sixteen. When the four composition titles have been agreed on,

the two groups come together as a class to reselect four titles from eight. Discussion follows, the teacher arbitrating if necessary. The four titles the class finally selects are then set as a 'mock' examination or a timed two-hour homework.

3 If the Book option has been prepared, students are advised to choose question 5. Many of the activities suggested on pp51–5 can be adapted to answer this question. The differences between question 5 and the practice given on pp51–5 lie in the use of tenses. Instead of writing narrative in the past tense, it is more customary for accounts of books to be written in the present simple. Although the past tense would not be incorrect in answering questions such as:

> 'The two funerals in this story are both for Harry Lime. Explain how this occurred.'

students should realise the Present Simple is more usual and natural, and be given practice in using it for book commentaries.

CHAPTER 3

Paper 3
The Use Of English

GENERAL DESCRIPTION

The main aim of this paper is to test candidates' knowledge of English grammar. It has two sections: the first is very controlled and asks candidates to perform certain tasks such as rewording sentences, writing sentences from notes and filling in gaps in texts. In these types of exercise the number of possible answers is normally limited. The second section concentrates on directed writing – students will normally have to read a text and summarise the contents, often involving expressing opinions, giving advice or making suggestions.

Clearly, the first part of this paper requires candidates to demonstrate their ability to manipulate the language according to the grammatical rules they have learned. It is possible to predict most of the structures and functions which candidates will be expected to know, bearing in mind that this is an examination for intermediate learners, and these will be listed on pp65–6.

The second part of the paper requires candidates to be familiar with various styles of written English such as job, accommodation and holiday advertisements and descriptions, or extracts from books and newspapers. A typical text may also give information about three or four people and ask candidates to choose the best job, flat, holiday, newspaper, etc, for each one. It is therefore necessary for students to understand the information given in the text in order to make a reasonable choice, and then express it in accurate English.

Information available on the Use of English marking scheme is limited. The Handbook refers to 'Paper 3 as being marked out of a working total arrived at during the examiners' meeting. This is then scaled down to a total of 40 marks.'

No doubt it is difficult for the Board to be more specific, as there are many sections to this particular paper, and much variety within the number and types of questions which may be set. Once again one should bear in mind the Board's intention to view the examination as a whole rather than a sum of its individual parts.

CONTENTS OF INDIVIDUAL SECTIONS

There are usually five or six questions in the Use of English paper. The types of question which may be expected are as follows:

A cloze passage

This is usually a text of between 200 and 250 words, often describing a person, event or scene, with twenty gaps each of which must be filled with one word. The missing words are normally elements of grammar such as nouns, verbs, adjectives, prepositions, pronouns, articles, conjunctions. Here is an example:

> 'Jane Brown is typical of many mothers in Britain today. Although she has a young child and (1) .... like to be at home to look (2) .... her, she has to supplement the family (3) .... with a part-time job. (4) .... husband, Peter, was unemployed (5) .... fifteen months before (6) .... a job two months (7) .... as a clerk in an office.'

Sentence transformation

This question usually consists of ten sentences which have to be rewritten, beginning with the words given, so that they mean exactly the same as the original sentence. Here are five examples:

1 I haven't had so much fun for a long time.
It's a long time..

2 It isn't necessary for you to work until 6 pm.
You ....

3 Ann stayed away from work because she was ill.
If she ....

4 I would prefer you to deliver the table on Saturday.
I would rather ....

5 The TV company is making a film about China.
A film ....

Vocabulary

There are three types of questions which may appear in this section of the paper. All usually test knowledge of a) phrasal verbs, and their conjugation in the context of a sentence, b) transformation of words ie, adjectives to nouns and c) word families. Here are some examples of each type:

1 Fill each blank with a phrase made from GO

a You will have to .... this letter again because it's full of mistakes.

b That shop is so expensive the price of butter .... almost every week.

c The cheese smells terrible. It must have ....

2 The word at the end of each of the following sentences can be used to form a word that fits suitably in the blank space. Fill each blank in this way:

a She said 'Hello' in a .... way. (FRIEND)

b My parents .... me to learn to drive. (COURAGE)

c Ten thousand people have been made .... by the earthquake. (HOME)

3 Complete the following sentences with one appropriate word connected with the subject of 'Money':

a We'd rather you didn't pay by cheque or credit card. We usually only accept ....

b What is the .... rate of the dollar this week?

c During the sale the shop will give a 25 per cent .... on all purchases over £200.

All three of the above types of vocabulary testing have been analysed on pp8–10 in connection with Section A of the Reading Comprehension paper.

Incomplete dialogue

This question requires candidates to complete a dialogue between two people. The missing sentences or utterances are usually questions, which means that students must read and understand the answers in order to establish what the questions are. Ability to have accurate control over various kinds of question formations is thus necessary for this part of the examination. Here is an example:

A: Amazon Travel Services. Can I help you?
B: Yes, thank you. I would like to go to Barcelona as soon as possible. When .... ?
A: There will be a flight tomorrow at 11.30.
B: Are .... ?
A: Yes, sir. The flight is not yet fully booked.
B: What.................................... ?
A: A single ticket is £95.
B: Can...................................... ?
A: Certainly, sir. Two tickets for flight no. BP396.

Letter from notes

In this question candidates are expected to read ten sentences in note form which together make up a letter. They have to make complete and accurate sentences from the notes, remembering that the sentences form a single letter and therefore relate to each other. The kinds of alteration which need to be made are verb conjugations and inclusion of articles, prepositions, conjunctions, pronouns, etc. However, the notes are given in the correct word order, so no other rearrangements are necessary. Here are some example sentences:

Dear Sir,

a I / annoyed / letter / I receive / you this morning
b In it / I not pay / cassette / sent / last month
c You say / I / pay immediately
d In fact / I send back / cassette / you / same day / receive
e I return / because / not like

Paragraph writing

This final question requires candidates to read and understand one or more texts and to write paragraphs giving opinions or advice based on the information given. After the Composition paper, this is the closest candidates come in the examination to writing connected discourse. Summary and collating skills are involved here, as well as a limited degree of creative thinking. An example of this type of question is as follows:

The following four people are travelling on an aeroplane, reading different newspapers and magazines. Using the information given, continue paragraphs 1–4 in about 50 words each.

Name	Age	Family	Job	Interests
Jean Turner	46	Married, 2 children: Peter (garage mechanic), Susan (hairdressing school)	Assistant in a bakery	Dressmaking, knitting, socialising with friends, reading
Paul Kelly	53	Married, 2 grown up children	Estate Agent	The Stock Market. Shooting and fishing. Renovating his country house
Bill Lewis	24	Single. Lives with parents	Bus driver	Football and betting on horses. Discos and pubs
Margaret Wilson	30	Recently married	Doctor	Classical music. Member of local political group. Theatre. Country walking

Newspapers and magazines:

The Daily Satellite	**The Market Place**	**Women of Today**	**Popular People**
Top Pop Charts	The Dollar – current rates	Wife or careerist?	Royal babies
Win your next holiday in the sun	Investment advice	Mozart festival	Knit the perfect sweater
All the sports results	Country living	Hills and mountains	Household hints for coffee mornings
Film star's secret lover	Home improvements	The Political Woman	This month's novel selection

1. I think Jean Turner is reading ....
2. Paul Kelly is reading ....
3. Bill Lewis prefers ....
4. Margaret Wilson is the kind of person who reads ....

BREAKDOWN OF SKILLS NEEDED

From an analysis of language aspects tested in Paper 3, it is possible to predict most of the structures and functions that a student needs to be familiar with in order to answer the questions, bearing in mind that five of the six question types usually set are concerned with accurate and controlled use of English grammar. This section will list some of the major areas which are normally tested in Paper 3 but we must stress, that the following is in no way a syllabus but merely a reference list for the teacher. In order to successfully complete Paper 3, a candidate will need to have a reasonably accurate control over the following:

STRUCTURES

Tenses:

present simple and present continuous / present perfect simple and present perfect continuous / past simple and past continuous / past perfect simple and past perfect continuous / used to / future simple and future continuous / future perfect / present continuous for the future / going to

and

passives
conditionals
reported speech
modal verbs
gerunds and infinitives
adjectives and adverbs – comparatives and superlatives
relative clauses

FUNCTIONS

Expressions of:

preference
request
advice
suggestion
invitation
acceptance and refusal of invitation
regret
prediction
criticism
explanation
pros and cons
similarities and differences

A question-by-question breakdown of skills that students need to be able to perform on Paper 3 is as follows:

1 The Cloze Test

This requires candidates to:

- understand cohesive elements in text and dialogue
- utilise all the skills necessary for reading comprehension, as outlined on pp11–12
- recognise different parts of speech

2 Sentence transformation

This requires students to manipulate different parts of speech in order to produce sentences with different structures but the same meaning.

3 Vocabulary or Incomplete dialogue

Vocabulary requires candidates to:

- be familiar with phrasal verbs and their conjugations in the context of a sentence
- be able to form nouns from verbs, adjectives from adverbs, verbs from nouns, etc
- be aware of thematically based word families.

Incomplete dialogue requires candidates to:

- understand elements that make up connected spoken discourse
- be able to make questions from answers.

4 Letter from notes

This requires candidates to:

- understand information given in note form
- recognise key words which provide clues as to verb tenses
- be able to manipulate prepositions, articles, conjunctions, pronouns, etc, in order to make cohesive sentences.

5 Paragraph writing

This requires candidates to:

- utilise all the skills necessary for reading comprehension. See pp11–12
- express opinions based on reasoned understanding of a text
- practise summary skills.

SUGGESTED CLASSROOM ACTIVITIES

Cloze texts

As mentioned on p62, the missing words in the cloze passage are normally nouns, verbs, adjectives, pronouns, articles, prepositions and conjunctions. The following activities are to familiarise students with the different parts of speech so that they can more easily find suitable words to fill the gaps.

1 The teacher draws a grid on the board as follows:

noun	verb	adjective	adverb	pronoun	article	preposition

The class is then 'brainstormed' for examples of each type of word and the teacher writes a short list of words on the board under each heading:

noun	verb	adjective	adverb	pronoun	article	preposition
cat house bag	go buy see	old big cheap	quickly well softly	my him hers	the a an	to with by

Students then work in pairs to make sentences using the words in the grid, changing the verb form where necessary. This could be treated as a competition to see who can make the longest sentence. Sentences are then read aloud and the class can comment as to whether they are grammatically correct and semantically meaningful. An example from this grid might be:

'My old cat has gone with him to see the big house'

which is grammatically correct and might even mean something in a particular situation!

2 The teacher writes on the board or dictates a list of words which students then put into a grid like the one in the previous exercise. Then, as before, they make sentences in pairs using the words – this time the competition could be to see which pair has the greatest number of correct sentences after each one has been heard and checked for accuracy.

3 The teacher writes a sentence on the board and calls out one word which students have to replace as quickly as possible with a suitable (ie grammatically correct and meaningful) alternative. For example:

'My expensive camera has been stolen from my car'.

If the teacher calls out 'expensive' students could call out or write down 'new', 'favourite', 'Russian', etc, with points given to the quickest student and the students who think of words no one else has thought of. Similarly, 'stolen' could be replaced by 'taken', 'camera' by 'wallet', 'car' by 'bag', 'my' by 'her'.

4 The teacher writes two lists of half sentences on the board:

A	**B**
It rained	he liked football too
We were late	she thought she wouldn't enjoy it
He said he liked tennis	we had to cancel the picnic
She had a good time	the film hadn't started

Students have to find the second part in B to the phrase in list A and think of a word that links the two together, eg, 'so', 'but', 'and', 'although'. Then, in pairs, students make up their own sentences and on a second sheet of paper, write only the first part of the sentence (as in list A above), which they then exchange with another pair who try to guess how the sentence finishes. The two pairs then get together and see how close their ideas are to the original. The activity can then be repeated with pairs writing the second half of sentences, including the conjunction:

eg: ....so we all went home.
...........................but it was terrible!

The other pair then have to try to guess what the first part of the sentence was. (See p41.)

5 Phrasal and prepositional verbs need to be practised as these are often tested in the Cloze passage. Ideas for classroom practice are given on pp20–3. The remainder of the suggestions concentrate more specifically on the task of completing a Cloze text.

6 Each student in the class is given the same Cloze passage to read, and is asked to do so in five minutes. Then in pairs, the general theme of the text is discussed – what it is about overall. The object is for students to obtain as much information as possible from the context, without worrying about what the missing words are. There can follow a class discussion and a pooling of ideas as to what the text is about. This can be done with a variety of texts and the gaps can then be filled by students for homework and compared and corrected the next day.

7 Students are given short texts to read with a partner. Half the class are given one text and the other half another. Pairs then block out one particular part of speech throughout their text, eg all the adjectives, keeping a copy of the original for later reference. Pairs now exchange texts and discuss with their partners the possible words that could be used to fill the spaces. When they have filled them in, they form new pairs and check their answers with a student who has the original. Discussion then follows first in pairs, then as a class, as to whether the various possibilities that have been selected are suitable or not.

8 The Cloze type practice as explained on p19 is also relevant here. Once they are familiar with this activity, students can be encouraged to prepare their own passages to try out on the rest of the class, which may lead to discussions about word classes and why some types of gap are more difficult to fill than others.

9 Students prepare their own Cloze passages by selecting texts and blanking out twenty words of different types. They then get into pairs, exchange texts, complete the one they have been given and discuss their choices of words with the students who 'set' their task for them.

10 For further practice of all the above, students can now be given Cloze texts from past examination papers to discuss in pairs – first, the subject of the passage, then the types of words missing and lastly suggestions as to what these words could be. They then compare their answers with other students and finally the whole class can contribute to a 'model' answer which the teacher writes on the board.

Sentence transformation

When the teacher introduces any new grammatical structure, it is useful to encourage students to build up their own grammar reference notes, grouping together example sentences which have the same meaning expressed in a different way. If students can refer to English definitions rather than translations when they are revising, they are more likely to become familiar with the task of transforming sentences. If the teacher presents different aspects of the same structure at different times, asking students where this fits into their notes and letting them add examples on the same page is a useful way of sensitising them to the fact that there is more than one grammatical way of expressing the same idea. These notes can later be referred to whenever necessary. 'John is taller than Peter' and 'Peter isn't as tall as John' are examples. Even if these are taught at different times, the teacher can ask students where the second structure fits into their notes, give them time to make similar pairs of examples, and later use these alternative sentences for the activity on p72. Suggestions for types of transformations which can occur follow. It must be stressed that this list is based on an analysis of past papers and is not meant as a definitive syllabus.

a The train is full of people.
b There are a lot of people on the train.

a That film is fantastic!
b What a fantastic film!

a London is bigger than Oxford.
b Oxford is smaller than London.
c Oxford isn't as big as London.

a There are more girls than boys here.
b There aren't as many boys as girls here.

a He was the fastest runner.
b No one ran as fast as him.

a Smoking is bad for you.
b It is bad for you to smoke.

a I prefer staying in to going out.
b I'd rather stay in than go out.

a 'I'll be there at nine' she said to me.
b She told me that she would be there at nine.

a They repaired my car at the garage in town.
b I had my car repaired at the garage in town.

a I was silly to say that.
b I am sorry I said that.
c I wish I hadn't said that.
d I regret having said that.
e I shouldn't have said that.

a Both Mary and Peter prefer jazz to classical music.
b Neither Mary nor Peter prefers classical music to jazz.

a Who was to blame?
b Whose fault was it?

a We worked hard so that we would finish quickly.
b We worked hard in order to finish quickly.

a We used to live in Athens.
b We don't live in Athens any more.

a He plays tennis as well as football.
b Not only does he play tennis but he plays football too.

a As soon as she arrived home the telephone rang.
b No sooner had she arrived home than the telephone rang.

a It's a five minute drive.
b It takes five minutes to drive there.

a He's too old to get the job.
b He isn't young enough to get the job.

a Although the weather was bad, we had a good time.
b Despite the bad weather, we had a good time.

a I haven't seen you for ages.
b It's ages since I saw you.
c The last time I saw you was ages ago.

a How long is it since I last saw you?
b When did I last see you?

a This is the first time I've ever been here.
b I've never been here before.
c I haven't ever been here before.

a She sings so well that everyone buys her records.
b She's such a good singer that everyone buys her records.

a I advise you to buy it.
b If I were you, I'd buy it.
c I suggest you buy it.
d Why don't you buy it?

1 A variation and extension of the idea on p36 is useful and relevant here: The class divides into groups and each group is given ten small cards. The teacher reads a sentence aloud and students decide in their groups if it is grammatically correct, or not. If the whole group agrees that it is correct they 'bet' one card – if they are right, they win another card, if wrong they lose one. For instance the teacher reads out 'I haven't seen you for ages'. Groups A and C think it's correct, groups B and D decide it's incorrect. After every group has announced its decision the teacher gives a card to groups A and C and takes one from groups B and D. In the case of an incorrect sentence, an extra card can be given to the first group to correct it. For example, 'I never was here before' should be 'I've never been here before'. Finally, a 'bonus' card can be given to the first group to give a different sentence which means the same, in this case, 'This is the first time I've ever been here'.

2 Students divide into groups of three or four. The teacher gives two sets of cards to each group. On each card of one set is written a complete sentence. On each card of the other set there is one word. The first set is spread out face down on one table and the same is done with the second set on another. In turn students select one card from each set.

eg:

There are more girls than boys here	+	What...............

and decide if it is possible to make a sentence beginning with the word on the second card that means the same as the sentence on the first. Here it is not possible, so the cards are replaced face down. However, if the next student picks up 'That film is fantastic' he may remember where 'What...............' is, pick up that card and so make 'What a fantastic film!' keeping the cards.

3 Students can repeat the activities above by creating their own cards from lists of similar sentences they have 'collected' in the way we suggested earlier. Or, if this is felt to be too time-consuming and difficult, students simply test each other in pairs or small groups.

Vocabulary items

Pages 13–23 cover activities to practise for all three types of question in Paper 3 of the examination – ie phrasal verbs, adjective/noun/verb relationships, word families. In addition, we suggest that one of the best ways of building up students' vocabulary generally is to encourage them to read as much as possible, using an English-English dictionary rather than a translating one.

Incomplete dialogues

1 Students form groups. Each group is given a number of cards with basic short answers to 'Yes/No' questions, eg 'Yes, I have', 'No, he didn't'. The teacher reads out a question, for instance, 'Did John do his homework yesterday?' and the first group to find a card with a suitable answer, eg 'Yes, he did' gives it to the teacher. The first group to get rid of all its cards is the winner.

2 As above, but this time the students are given cards with questions on and the teacher reads an answer. The groups have to find a question to which the answer would be suitable. If, for instance, the teacher says, 'Yes, I have', a suitable card might read 'Have you ever been to Spain?'

3 When students are familiar with basic short answer forms, similar activities can be carried out with less straightforward answers. For example, if the teacher's question is 'Does Susan live in New York?' the students may have to find a card which says 'She did, but she's in Toronto now'. Equally, the teacher may read out the answer, 'Well, I prefer the theatre' and the students may have to look for a question such as 'Do you often go to the cinema?'

4 The teacher writes a word on the board and gives the class a limited time to write down as many questions as possible to which the word could be the answer. For example, 'London' is the word. Possible questions could be 'Where do you live/work/come from?', 'Where were you born?', 'Where did you go yesterday?', 'What's your favourite city?', etc. The teacher then adds a preposition to the word, 'in London' and students discuss in pairs which of the above questions are still possible, – here the first two would be possible, the last two would not. In the case of the impossible ones, they can now decide which prepositions, if any, are needed to make them possible, for example 'to' in the case of 'Where did you go yesterday?' and '(nothing)' in answer to 'What's your favourite city?'.

5 Sets of cards could be made to practise short answer forms to information questions like those above. Half the cards in each set would have questions written on them, eg 'Who were you talking to last night?', 'Where did he go yesterday?', 'Who did she marry?', 'Where did you meet your boyfriend?', 'How do you get to the station?', and the other half would have short answers, both with and without prepositions, eg 'to Peter', 'to the cinema', 'Peter', 'at Gatwick Airport', 'by bus'. Students form groups. The pile of question cards is placed in the middle of the table. Each student is given six answer cards. Students take turns to pick a card from the question pile read it aloud to the group and return it to the bottom of the pile. Everyone looks to see if they have an answer to it in their hand. If anyone has, he reads it out and keeps both cards. The winner is the student who has the most pairs of correctly matched questions and answers.

6 The teacher writes a list of conversation initiators on the board, concentrating on functional areas such as inviting, suggesting, asking permission, offering, asking for advice (note, these are all question forms). These questions should be numbered from one to ten. Here is a suggested list:

1 Would you like to come to lunch on Saturday?
2 Why don't we go to the cinema?
3 Would you like a cup of tea?
4 Can I help you?
5 Do you mind if I sit here?
6 Could you help me put my case on the rack?
7 What time does the train leave, please?

8 What shall I do? I've lost my cat.
9 Have you got the time, please?
10 Could you feed my fish while I'm on holiday, please?

The teacher then dictates to the class a mixed up list of twelve possible responses to these initiators (including two distractors which do not fit with any of the questions). These should not be too obvious, in order to promote discussion. Students match up initiators and responses. Here this list would be:

A I'll help you look for it.
B No, I'm not.
C Yes, I'd love one.
D Yes, how often?
E Sorry, but I'm doing something then.
F Not too bad.
G At 10 o'clock.
H I'm a bit tired.
I Sorry, I haven't.
J Yes, I've lost my cat.
K Not at all.
L Yes, certainly.

(Answers are: 1–E; 2–H; 3–C; 4–J; 5–K; 6–L; 7–G; 8–A; 9–I; 10–D. (B and F are distractors)

7 When the initiators and responses have been matched up correctly (students can work in pairs before the class discusses the best answers) the teacher allocates a different pair of sentences to each pair of students, eg 4 – 'Can I help you?', J – 'Yes, I've lost my cat', and asks them to develop it into a longer dialogue which they will write, with the teacher monitoring, and then perform to the class.

In order to do this, students will have to decide who is speaking, eg 'cat owner' and 'policeman' and then decide how the dialogue develops. The teacher can limit the length to 8 or 10 lines. In this case a model dialogue might read:

S1: Can I help you?
S2: Yes, I've lost my cat.
S1: When did you last see it?
S2: Two days ago.
S1: What does it look like?
S2: It's black and white and quite big.
S1: I'll let you know if anyone finds it.
S2: Thank you.

8 Students are each given a card which says

Find someone in the class who .... eg likes tea / slept for more than seven hours last night / had eggs for breakfast this morning / owns a record by David Bowie / etc

They are given time to work out how to ask the various questions. If each card contains the same basic question types, the teacher can use one card as an example and chair a class discussion as to what the necessary question forms are. For instance:

> Where do you (come from?) / Do you (like tea?) / Can you (ski?) / What did you . . ? / Have you got . . ? / Did you . . ? / Do you . . ?

Students then walk around and ask each other their questions, getting any person who responds positively to a question to sign their name on the card. The first student with positive responses to all his questions is the winner, although all can be given time to try to finish.

9 The teacher writes a dialogue between two people, then writes each part of the dialogue on a separate card. Students move their chairs into a circle (with large classes more than one circle and set of cards may be required, but there should be a minimum of twelve and a maximum of sixteen). Each student is given a card containing part of the dialogue but the cards are handed out in a random order. The students must then memorise what is on their card and, in turn, say it aloud to the rest of the group. This may sound as follows:

S1: For some people.
S2: How's work?
S3: Majorca. Have you ever been there?
S4: So do I.
S5: No, I've just arrived.
S6: I hope so.
S7: Still, it will soon be holiday time.
S8: Shall we go to the cafe on the corner?
S9: Yes, in 1985. You'll like it.
S10: Aren't you having one then?
S11: Busy as usual. I hate Mondays.
S12: That's a good idea.
S13: Sorry, I'm late. Have you been here long?
S14: Not this year. Where are you going?

Students then have to physically arrange themselves into the correct order by changing places with each other. The teacher should collect the cards once they have been memorised so that the students are obliged to discuss as a group where they would sit, asking each other to repeat what was on their card when necessary. Eventually, they should be sitting so that the conversation sounds as follows, running clockwise round the circle:

S1: Sorry, I'm late. Have you been here long?
S2: No, I've just arrived.
S3: Shall we go to the cafe on the corner?
S4: That's a good idea.
S5: How's work?
S6: Busy as usual. I hate Mondays.
S7: So do I.
S8: Still, it will soon be holiday time.
S9: For some people!

S10: Aren't you having one then?
S11: Not this year. Where are you going?
S12: Majorca. Have you ever been there?
S13: Yes, in 1985. You'll like it.
S14: I hope so.

10 Students look at written dialogues with missing questions and discuss first in pairs and then in groups, what the questions could be, remembering to read the whole gapped dialogue first so as to be familiar with the context. Each group then gives their decision as to the best question for each space, and the teacher writes their choices on the board to initiate class discussion about which ones are the best and why.

11 Students work in pairs. The teacher gives each pair a situation,

eg Shopkeeper and customer in a shop / Travel agent and client in a travel agency / Two old friends who meet in the street

Students then work in pairs to write a short dialogue, using the given situation. The teacher checks for accuracy and students then write a second copy of their dialogue with the questions missing, except for the first word of each (the Examination length is usually six missing Questions). Pairs then exchange dialogues, fill in the missing questions and discuss their answers with the writers of the original. At this point pairs can help each other with hints, if necessary, but they may find that the questions chosen are quite suitable, even if they are not the same as the original, and this should provoke discussion.

Writing a letter from notes

1 Pairs of students are each given a letter from notes as in the Use of English paper. Their first task is to write a one sentence summary of the letter and what it is about, eg 'A letter from a friend to a friend describing a recent move to a new house', 'a letter of complaint from a customer to a shop about a faulty product', 'a letter of application for a job as office clerk'.

Letters are passed around from one pair to another so that each pair sees each letter. For the purposes of comparing one sentence summaries in whole class discussion, each letter can be given a number on the back.

2 Students look at examples of letters written in note form and underline any word in each sentence which may give them a clue as to which tense should be used. Here are three examples:

1 recently complete / two year course / tourism.
'Recently' informs students that the Present Perfect tense should be used here.

2 When we last meet / we tell you / we plan / move.
'Last' informs students that here the Past Simple should be used.

3 We / have a party / next Saturday
'Next Saturday' is a future time indicator, very often, as here, indicating something already arranged, thus indicating the Present Continuous for future plans.

After they have compared with a partner, and agreed on the tense for each sentence they can try to write the complete sentence, including the missing articles, pronouns and prepositions.

3 Students can be given a picture story such as the one on p43. They must then imagine that they are one of the characters in the story, and are writing to a friend describing what happened to them. Students must begin and end the letter with the usual expressions of greeting and leave-taking such as 'Thank you for your letter which I received yesterday' and 'I'm looking forward to seeing you'.

As we have seen, picture stories may be approached in various ways. If the method suggested on p44 is taken with students putting cut-up pictures into their correct order, they can write the story as a letter from one of the character's points of view.

4 ■ For further practice in extending sentences from notes, the teacher can give the class a short lecture – preferably about an experience told in the first person. The lecture should be given at normal speed and students asked to take notes. Clearly, they won't have time to write whole sentences, so they will have to choose what they consider to be the important information-prepositions, articles, pronouns are not usually important in notes. Students compare their own notes with their partner's, and, if necessary, the teacher repeats the lecture. Students compare again and collate all the information they have between them. A tape could also be used here instead of the teacher herself.

Finally, in pairs, students write up the information they have noted, in complete sentences. Sentences are read aloud and the teacher writes on the board the various attempts at reproducing each part of the lecture. Class discussion as to which is the best can follow.

5 Students form pairs, A and B. Student A then goes outside the room to listen to the teacher (who is outside) and who proceeds to read out a short text. When each student has retained as many words as possible, he goes back into the classroom and reports what he has heard to student B. Student B writes down from A's dictation. Student A then goes back outside for more, repeatedly reporting to his partner as much as he is able to remember. The first pair to finish are the winners but first they must be shown the original text to check for accuracy.

In larger classes, copies of the text can be pinned up on the wall in various parts of the room, and student A has to go to read it before dictating what he remembers to his partner.

Clearly, most students will remember only the key words in each sentence and will then have to decide, with their partners, what the correct tense must be, and where the articles, prepositions and pronouns go – in other words, they are building up a complete text from notes.

6 ■ Each pair finds or writes a complete letter of about ten sentences, and reduces the sentences to note form, ie by putting all verbs into their infinitive forms and taking out articles, prepositions, pronouns. Keeping a copy of the original letter, they exchange the notes they have written with another pair and try to write the complete sentences of the one they have received. In doing this pairs should remember the following procedure:

a read the whole set of notes to establish what the letter is about
b underline key words in each sentence to establish which tenses need to be used and
c decide where and which prepositions, articles and pronouns are needed.

When the letters have been completed the two pairs can get together and compare their answers with the original, discussing difficulties and discrepancies as they do so.

Paragraph writing and summarising

The majority of these questions require students to assimilate information about people – their character, likes and dislikes, age, experiences etc – and to choose jobs, holidays, presents, entertainment, books, etc, for them. The following activities prepare students for this task.

1 Each pair of students looks at a picture of a person, preferably a photograph, and tries to imagine something about the person's background and character. They write down a few words and phrases of description. They then have to select the following for each person in the picture:

a job / a holiday / a newspaper / a book / a place to spend an evening / a house / an ideal partner / a pet / a hobby

They describe each and note the reasons for their choice. They then join another pair and explain their choices and reasons.

2 Students are divided into groups of four and each one is given a card with a role on it. The card gives the student a name, age, job, personality, hobby etc. Students spend a few minutes thinking themselves into their role. In the centre of the table are placed four cards describing books or holidays or Christmas presents or competition prizes, etc, and each student has to decide which one he would like and present his case to the others.

3 Students divide into groups of three. Half the groups in the class are given the role of job applicants and the other groups are the interview panels. The teacher writes a job advertisement on the board

eg:

> **Tourist guide required for central Milan.**
> Must speak fluent English and have good knowledge of Italian and French.
> Applicants should be over 20 years old and with at least two years' experience of working with people.

In their groups of three the interviewers prepare the questions they will ask and the interviewees prepare what they will say about themselves and any questions they want to ask about the company. Each panel of interviewers then proceeds to interview three applicants, one by one. Afterwards the interviewers discuss who they will choose while the interviewees discuss with each other how they think they performed. Finally, each panel informs the applicants of their choice and the reasons for it. Written work about the proceedings and the invidivual student's experience of them follows for homework.

4 Students divide into groups of three, four or five and each person is given a role card. This time the group represent flatmates who are looking for another person to share their flat. The cards given out should state their personal habits around the house, eg do they smoke, play loud music, tend to go early to bed, share the cooking and housework, are they tidy, do they enjoy shopping, etc.

Another group of students is formed, the number depending on the number of flat groups. Each of these students is also given a role play card describing himself. These students will then visit each flat in turn – every, say, five minutes the teacher announces that it's time to move on – and after doing so, discuss which flat they'd like to move into. Meanwhile, the groups of flatmates discuss which of the applicants they would like to invite to share their flat. Each flat announces its decision in turn to the class and certain compromises might be necessary in order to accommodate all the students looking for a home. Various kinds of written work could follow for homework. Possible titles might include:

> A letter to a friend describing the 'interview' / The people I met today. / My choice and the reasons for it.

5 The class is to represent a local council discussing how to spend a fixed sum of money which has been allocated to improve the town's facilities. Groups are formed, each group preparing an argument as to how to spend the money in a certain way.

eg:
- group 1 .... on public transport and roads
- group 2 .... on sports facilities
- group 3 .... on cultural facilities
- group 4 .... on green spaces
- group 5 .... on entertainment and leisure
- group 6 .... on renovating old buildings

When they have prepared their arguments, new groups form comprising one student from each of the original groups in each new group. Each student then has to argue his case and a decision must be reached as to how the money will be spent. Once again written work follows for homework.

6 The whole class is given a map and information about tourist attractions in a particular town or area. Groups of four or five students are then formed and each group is given information about one member of a family who will be driving through the area for a day.

eg: grandmother who isn't able to walk far
mother who is very active and energetic
father who is tired of driving and likes visiting places of historical and cultural interest
James, aged 10, who is easily bored
Julie, aged 8, who suffers from hay fever

More information can be supplied about each person.

Each group then must decide which places the character they have been given would like to visit, and why. New groups are then formed, comprising one student from each of the original groups, and each member of the family has to put forward a case for the places they want to visit – compromises may be made, and individuals may decide to spend part of the day alone if this seems necessary. Once again, a written account of the proceedings follows for homework.

CHAPTER 4

Paper 4
Listening Comprehension

GENERAL DESCRIPTION

The Listening Comprehension paper consists of three, four or five authentic or simulated-authentic pieces of spoken English accompanied by comprehension questions of various kinds. Candidates often take the test on the same day as their oral examination. The test is pre-recorded onto a cassette which candidates listen to on a tape recorder. Much of their written activity consists of putting a tick in the correct box or, at most, writing times, dates, names, etc, along a dotted line. They rarely, if ever, need to write a complete sentence. Students hear each taped item twice. The test lasts approximately thirty minutes.

CONTENTS OF INDIVIDUAL SECTIONS

The sections of this paper are the different taped extracts. These include conversations in specific situations, announcements, advertisements, various kinds of information giving radio news, formal talks, interviews and other types of broadcast material. Testing devices vary from extract to extract: multiple choice, true/false, gap-filling, matching information, and reordering information have been employed during the last four years and are likely to remain standard testing procedures for the forseeable future. The passages are usually spoken quite clearly, although candidates may have to deal with background noise and local accents.

Examples of questions are the following:

1 Multiple choice

Students are asked to select one of four possible answers to questions about the tape. These questions can be general, testing understanding of the text as a whole, or specific, asking for details.

eg: You will hear a radio programme in which an author talks about a book she has written.
For each of the questions 2–5 tick (√) one of the boxes A, B, C or D to show correct answer.

2 What is the book about?

A how children learn to make friends. | A |
B the problems of children in cities. | B |
C a boy from an African family. | C |
D a girl who feels sad at living away from home. | D |

3 Who wrote the book?

A a business woman from Nigeria. | A |
B the wife of a Nigerian diplomat. | B |
C a woman who was born in Nigeria. | C |
D a Nigerian woman who married an Englishman. | D |

4 Why did she decide to write stories?

A She wanted to read them to her children. | A |
B Her children liked them so much. | B |
C So that they would not be forgotten. | C |
D Her son asked her to do so. | D |

5 What is a problem for Mory?

A No-one plays with him. | A |
B He doesn't like other children. | B |
C Other boys laugh at him. | C |
D His father doesn't talk to him much. | D |

2 True/false questions

Here students are asked to indicate whether a series of statements made about the extract are true or false. A variation of this is when the question asks candidates to study a list and tick only the information which they have heard. Examples of both kinds follow:

1. You will hear an advertisement for new houses.
For each of the questions 16–21 tick (√) one box to show whether the statements are true or false.

WHAT WE OFFER <u>YOU</u>

	True	*False*
16 many different styles of house	☐	☐
17 from two to five bedrooms	☐	☐
18 houses all over England	☐	☐
19 discount if you buy now	☐	☐
20 part exchange on your own home	☐	☐
21 all removal costs paid	☐	☐

LIVE IN A STYLISH HOME!

2. You will hear a conversation between two friends about preparing a meal. For question 1 tick (√) the boxes to show which items they need to get from the shop.

- cheese ☐
- eggs ☐
- bread ☐
- cream ☐
- rice ☐
- butter ☐
- chicken ☐
- beans ☐
- lemon ☐

3 Gap-filling

Here candidates listen to a passage which includes details such as dates, times, telephone numbers, places, activities, etc. They then have to complete a timetable, or programme of information sheet with the missing details.

eg: Someone is giving details about a programme to new students at a college. For questions 6–15 fill in the missing information on the revised timetable in the spaces provided.

PROGRAMME		
TIME 11.00 am (6).............	**PLACE** Main Hall (7)............. (Group A) (8)..............(Group B) (9)............. (Group C)	**ACTIVITY** Introductions Discussion in groups
12.00 pm	(10)	General discussion
1.30 pm (12)	Main Hall Dining Room	Lunch (11) .... (13) ....
(14) .... 4.30 pm	Assembly Room	Questions (15) ....

4 Matching information

This is a typical set of pictures which students have to study and then indicate which ones are being described.

eg: Put a tick (√) against the two women Jane Whitby describes.

5 Re-ordering information

This kind of question asks candidates to study a series of pictures or statements about a sequence of events, and to rearrange them in the order in which they happened, according to the speaker.

eg: A learner driver comes across various difficulties. In the boxes numbered 1–4 enter the letter for each difficulty in the order in which they happen.

With regard to the marking procedure for Paper 4, the Handbook says it carries a total of 20 marks out of the whole examination total of 180, and forms part of the

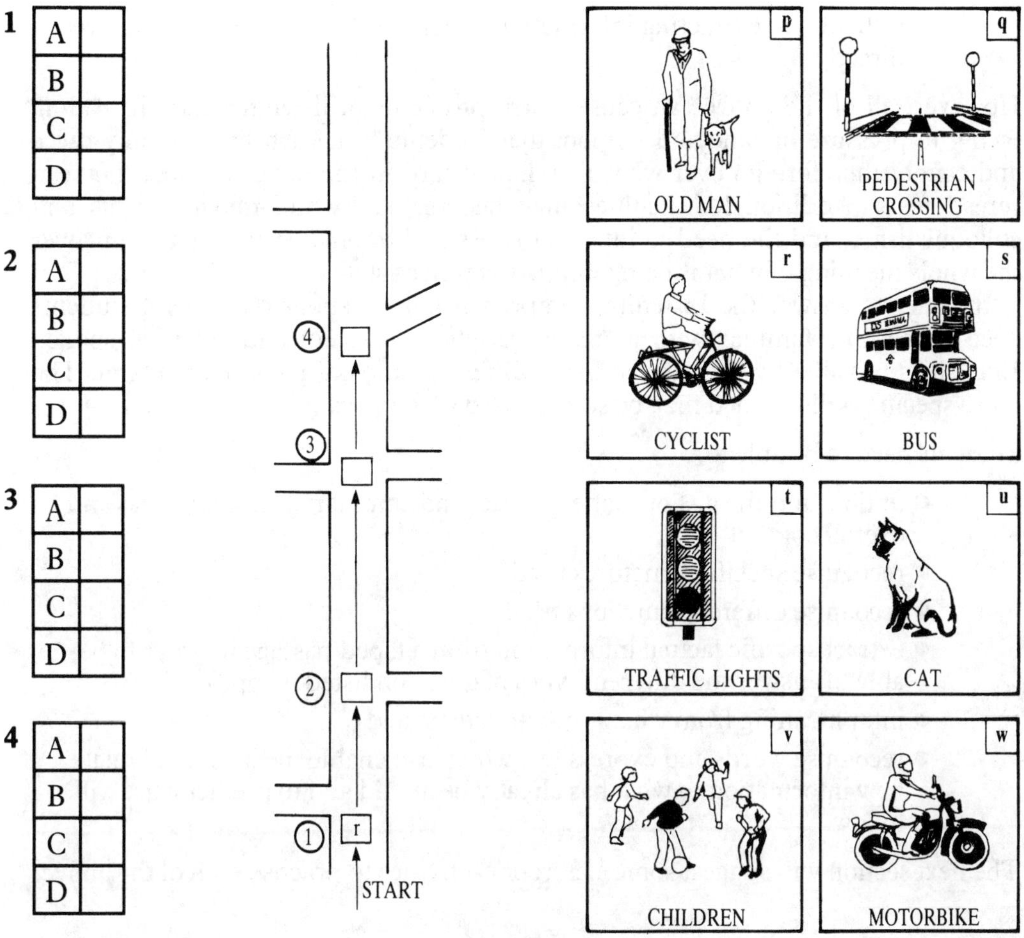

one-third aural/oral component of the examination.

This total of 20 for the paper may be adjusted up or down according to various administrative factors.

BREAKDOWN OF SKILLS NEEDED

Some of the most common problems that foreign students have when approaching listening comprehension can be likened to those listed on p12 with regard to Reading comprehension.

eg:
- difficulty in obtaining an initial overall impression due to a tendency to worry too soon about unfamiliar words and expressions
- difficulty at a later stage in extracting specific details from a mass of information

- difficulty in extracting information which is inferred rather than relayed directly

However, all of the above can cause worse problems in listening than in reading owing to pressure of time and the fact that students hear each passage only twice and cannot therefore go over what they have heard in the same way that they can reread texts. Additional difficulties may be created by unfamiliar accents and colloquialisms, and the need to interpret stress and intonation in order to uncover the whole meaning of what is being implied as well as stated.

In order to answer the Listening comprehension questions on Paper 4 students need to become familiar with as many varieties of accent and styles of spoken English as possible by listening to many different kinds of recorded material. The more specific skills needed may be summarised as follows:

Students need to be able to:

- understand the gist of a taped extract and summarise its main ideas and overall content
- recognise specific structures used
- recognise different functions used
- extract specific factual information from a taped passage in order to be able to answer the different types of question listed on pp81–87
- infer meaning from what is not directly stated
- recognise words and expressions which can enable the listener to relate new information to what has already been said and to predict what will follow

The next section will suggest some classroom activities to practise each of the above.

SUGGESTED CLASSROOM ACTIVITIES

Listening for gist

1 Activity 1 on p24 could be repeated for a tape instead of a reading passage.

2 A short extract is played to the class once, after which students individually answer the following questions which the teacher can write on the board for students to consider before the tape is played:

- What kind of passage is it? (eg an inverview, an advertisement, a radio extract, a news item, a friendly conversation, an announcement.)
- Who is speaking? (eg two friends, waiter and customer, husband and wife.)
- What is it about? (In *one* sentence, eg 'It's the weather forecast for tomorrow.' 'It's two friends discussing where to go tonight.' 'It's a station announcement about cancelled trains.')

Pairs compare and discuss their answers. The teacher repeats the exercise with other tapes and each time pairs compare and discuss. Finally, the class comes together and the answers to all the extracts are discussed. If there is disagreement the teacher plays the extract in question again and the students can discuss who is correct.

3 Students form groups of three. Each student is given six cards – student A has six phrases describing types of taped recording (eg a news item, a review of a book), student B has six descriptions of who is speaking (eg teacher to student) and student C has six sentences summarising passages (eg It's about a wedding in a registry office). The cards are all numbered 1–6 in the corner. The teacher now plays a tape of six short extracts and students write down the number of their card which refers to each one. This process is repeated twice more with the students changing cards on each occasion. All three students in each group will now have three pieces of information about each extract. They compare and discuss answers, and then a full class discussion takes place as to which cards refer to which extract.

4 The teacher selects six taped extracts to play to the class and prepares beforehand one multiple-choice question about the gist of each. As described on pp31–2, each question should have one correct answer, one impossible answer and two distractors which might be thought to be correct on first listening.

eg: The weather forecast in passage 1 tells us that tomorrow the weather will be:

A very good
B quite good
C not too good
D bad

or The description in passage 2 is about:

A a painting of an old house
B a piece of antique furniture found in an old house
C an old house full of antique furniture
D a painting of an antique table

Students listen to each extract once and individually find their answers, then compare them with their partner. Each extract is then played a second time and after each one, students discuss, in groups of four, which answer best sums up the text and why. Finally, the whole class discuss the correct answers to all six passages.

5 The whole class listens to a dialogue between two people and discusses who they are and what they are talking about, in general, eg 'a doctor and a patient discussing whether or not the latter should seek a second opinion about his condition'. Students are then divided into pairs and when the tape is played a second time student A makes brief notes each time the first speaker talks, and student B does the same for the second speaker. These notes should be some important words to help the students to remember the gist of the conversation. Pairs then write a short dialogue reproducing the gist of what was said on the tape.

Pairs then compare their conversations with that of another pair and check to see if they have included the same information. Finally, the class can contribute to a final version which the teacher writes on the board, discussing line by line whether the sentence summarises what was said on the tape. The teacher can play part of the tape again where there is disagreement.

6 Students form groups of four. The teacher plays a short passage and each group discusses the gist of it. They then write a true statement and a false statement about what they have heard, and indicate which is which.

eg: 'You can hear two friends planning a holiday' (T)
'You can hear two friends discussing their last holiday' (F)

The teacher monitors to ensure that groups have understood the gist. She then plays five more short extracts and the students repeat the above process for each. The teacher then plays the first extract a second time, and each group in turn reads their statements aloud and the other groups quietly discuss which is true and which is false. Groups then announce their decisions and the teacher awards points to the groups who have chosen correctly. The above is repeated for the other five passages. The winning group is the one with the most points.

7 The teacher plays a tape in which someone expresses an opinion about something. For instance, 'a teacher explains why she thinks that examinations should be abolished', 'a city dweller explains why he dislikes modern architecture', 'an unemployed person talks about what it is like to be without work'. Students are asked to note the main points of the argument as they listen the first time. They then form pairs and compare the number of points they have noted, and the main arguments put forward. They hear the passage a second time and then pairs join up to form groups of four. Discussion follows before groups write summaries of the extract. When the class comes together, groups give their summaries to the teacher, who writes them on the board. The whole class votes for the best-written summary.

■ Listening for structures

1 The teacher selects a short taped dialogue which concentrates on practising specific grammatical structures. For example, if conditionals are the focus, a taped dialogue can be the following:

S1: John? It's Susan. Would you like to come to dinner this evening?
S2: I'd love to but I can't. I've got to work late.
S1: But I haven't seen you for ages!
S2: I'd come if I could, really. Look, if I can get away by 8, I'll come.
S1: Please try . . . if it's not too dark I'll show you my new car.
S2: Okay. By the way, have you heard from Peter lately?

S1: No. He's in New York. He said he'd write if he had time, so he must be too busy.

S2: I'm busy myself right now. Look, I must go. If my boss hears me, he'll go on about running up large phone bills in the firm's time. I'll try and come round later.

S1: Okay. Bye.

The teacher plays the dialogue once while every student writes down the number of conditional sentences she hears, ie 5. They then compare as a class – the numbers are usually different. The second time the tape is played students raise their hands each time they hear a conditional sentence (or possibly, their left hand for a 1st conditional, their right for a 2nd – if, that is, the teacher wishes to make things more complicated!) Discussion follows once again as to how many examples of the structure the passage contains. The third time the tape is played the teacher stops the machine each time someone raises their hand and asks them to repeat the sentence they heard. This is written on the board exactly as the student says it. The class discusses and corrects. The final stage is for the teacher to write the dialogue on the board as a series of prompts.

eg: John? / Susan / dinner this evening?
love to / can't / work late.
but / haven't / you ages
come / could. / if / away by 8 / . . .

In pairs students write the dialogue before finally comparing their versions with that on the tape.

2 The teacher plays a short extract of a person speaking, and the class comments on which tense is being used in the main – is it a description of a past event, everyday routine, or future plans? The second time the extract is played students individually note as many words as they can that tell them about the tense – words like: yesterday; ago; last year; this year; nowadays; next month; tomorrow, etc, as well as verbs. In pairs they compare and then listen a second time to see if they can add more. Each pair then contributes its list to a collective list which the teacher writes on the board. The board can be divided into two – one side for time phrases, the other for verbs. In pairs again students now try to reproduce the passage, using the words on the board to help them remember. Finally, each pair in turn calls out a sentence for the teacher to write on the board and the class to comment on.

3 The communal dictation idea suggested on pp77–8 also gives valuable practice in listening for structures.

Listening for specific factual information

1 Bingo can be played to give students practice in listening for different kinds of number – dates, times, telephone numbers, etc. Each student is given a card divided into nine squares. In each square is written, eg a telephone number:

632–4418	314–5511	633–2297
633–448	217–9282	315–5511
311–5441	622–3397	217–8282

Each student is given a pile of blank cards to cover the numbers with. The teacher calls out a telephone number and if the student has the number on his card he covers it with a blank. The first student to cover all nine squares shouts 'Bingo' and everyone stops. Students then exchange their cards with their partners who check that the correct numbers have been covered, as the teacher writes each number she called on the board. The winner wins a point, students change cards and the game is repeated. Clearly it is better practice for students if several of the numbers on the cards are only slightly different. Similarly, for times (the same card could contain 10.15 and 10.50) or for dates (the same card could contain Tuesday 13th June and Tuesday 30th June).

2 On the board the teacher puts six pictures of people and proceeds to give factual information about each in a mixed up order. Students complete the following table as they listen:

	Person 1	**Person 2**	**Person 3**	**Person 4**	**Person 5**	**Person 6**
Name						
Date of birth						
Address						
Phone number						
Car						

The teacher says 'Person number 3 lives at 77 Briary Road, that's B–R–I–A–R–Y road', etc. Pairs compare their completed tables, before the whole class discuss correct answers.

3 The class is divided into three groups – A, B and C. Students in each group are given a different completed form related to a listening passage, eg a job application form with all the information stated in the actual interview included. Groups make up six of their own True or False sentences about the information they have in front of them.

eg: John was born on 20th June 1958.
He has worked in his present job for 3 years.
He speaks French . . .

Groups of three are now formed, with one student from each previous group in each. Student A dictates her six sentences to the other two who write them down. The teacher then plays the tape of the interview while B and C indicate if the sentences are True or False. The process is repeated by students B and C who each dictate their sentences to the others before the teacher plays the relevant taped extract. Groups then compare their answers and discuss differences before hearing each extract a second time and finally checking their answers with the student who prepared the questions.

4 Variations on the above can be used to practise multiple-choice and open-ended questions. Half the class are given transcript A and the other half transcript B. Using the information they have in front of them, pairs prepare six multiple-choice questions, as on p89, Activity 4.

eg: Mary is returning the radio to the shop because
A it doesn't work
B it's an unwanted present
C the quality of the sound is bad
D she's seen another one she likes better

or six open-ended questions:

'Why is Mary returning the radio?'
'Why did she buy it?'
etc . . .

Pairs then exchange lists of questions with a pair who have prepared questions on the other passage. The teacher plays both extracts once and students discuss their answers. The teacher plays both passages a second time. Pairs now form groups of four and check their answers with the students who prepared the questions.

5 Every student is given a map of a town centre and told that they are standing in a specific place, for example 'the station'. The teacher then gives directions to another building and students individually indicate on the map the building they arrive at when they follow the directions. Pairs compare answers and the reader repeats the instructions. The whole class then discuss the correct answer.

Students now form groups of four and each student in turn describes how to get to another building. The other three listen, then say which building they have arrived at, checking the answer with the student who gave the directions.

6 Students take a blank sheet of paper. The teacher describes a scene to the whole class, for example a street scene: 'There are two identical detached houses, each one with four windows, a chimney and a tree in the front garden to the left of the door. In front of the house to the left there is a car parked. The sun is shining. There are three people walking towards the church next to the house on the right. The church has a high spire.' Students draw a picture of what they hear. They then compare with partners. One student comes out to the board and asks different students to describe the picture they have drawn. He draws exactly what he hears on the board. The board picture should look the same as the teacher's original picture. As an extension of this each student now draws her own picture and describes it to her partner who draws what he hears – variations on the street scene can be furniture in a room, or a physical description of a person. Examples are:

> There is a bed behind the door, and an armchair under the window. Next to the bed is a small table with a square clock on it.
>
> or
>
> He's a tall man with short curly hair, a bushy beard and glasses. He's wearing check trousers and a striped blue and green sweater. He's carrying an umbrella in his right hand.

Students then compare their picture with the originals.

7 Students form groups of four. Each group is given the same set of picture cards, eg of people, houses, rooms, which they spread, face up, around the table. Each card has a number in the corner. The teacher then reads aloud a description of one of the pictures. The group discusses which picture has been described and one person writes down the number of that card. Several of the cards should have only slight differences, and the teacher could sometimes describe the same card twice in a slightly different way, to make it more challenging. Finally, the class report their answers to the teacher and discuss.

8 Students form pairs. Each pair is given twelve pictures which together make up a story. These pictures are spread around the table. A tape is then played, for example of a person describing an experience to a friend, and pairs arrange their pictures in the order in which the sequence of events occurred. They compare their order with another pair and then listen a second time to check. Finally, individuals in the class tell the story in what they believe is its correct chronological order, and the rest of the class agree or disagree with the ordering.

9 A variation on the above is when pairs are given a set of twelve cards with sentences on, again describing an experience. The sentences paraphrase exactly what is said on the tape so that students have to look for sentences that mean the same as what they hear. For instance, the speaker might say, 'Peter saw red when he got back to his car and found glass everywhere and his stereo missing'. The appropriate card would read, 'Peter was angry when he returned to find his car had been broken into'. Once again students listen to the tape and in pairs arrange the sentences into their chronological order. They compare their decision with that of another pair and listen again to the tape before class discussion takes place as to the correct order.

Inferential listening

1 Students need to be able to find out information that is not directly stated. The teacher plays a dialogue once and students discuss the following questions in pairs:

- Where are the speakers?
- What is their relationship to each other?
- What is the gist of the conversation?

Pairs then report their impressions to the rest of the class. The teacher then plays the tape a second time and students try to find out more about the speakers, this time discussing the following questions in groups of four:

- Do we know how old they are?
- Do we know anything about their occupations?
- Do we know anything else about their lives and backgrounds?
- What circumstances led to the present conversation?

Groups then report their impressions to the class and state how they arrived at them. Class discussion follows. The tape is then played a third time after which groups discuss the following:

- How do the speakers feel about each other during the conversation?
- How do they feel as a result of the conversation?

Groups report their impressions to the class.

2 The teacher writes an adjective on the board, such as 'angry'. She then plays a dialogue to the whole class. When students think that one of the speakers sounds angry, they raise their hands. The teacher stops the tape each time a hand is raised and asks the student to repeat what he heard that made him think the speaker was angry. The student tries to repeat the sentence in the same manner as it was spoken on the tape. The class decide if it is a good example of anger, or not. The teacher can then play the sentence or phrase repeatedly, allowing the whole class to practise the stress and intonation patterns used. Other examples of adjectives could be:

> nervous / surprised / aggressive / disappointed / hesitant / shy / sarcastic / upset

3 The teacher plays a dialogue and students, individually, note down single adjectives as they listen, describing the moods they sense in different parts of the dialogue. Pairs then compare the words they have written. The teacher plays the tape a second time, stopping at intervals to allow students to discuss the moods of the speakers at particular moments. Pairs then decide if the words they have chosen are still correct or whether there is a better word to more accurately describe the feeling. The whole class give their words to the teacher who writes them on the board. Students have to defend their choices of word if they are different from those the others have chosen. Finally, the class chooses a word or words to sum up the general mood of the conversation.

4 Although the following activity does not involve listening, it does sensitise students to mood and nuance.

Two students are asked to wait outside the classroom while the rest of the class choose an adverb which describes a manner of speaking or behaving. For example:

> lazily / enthusiastically / apprehensively / hurriedly / timidly / passionately

In the meantime the teacher askes a few quick questions around the class and students have to answer in the manner of the adverb they have decided on. – 'Would you like to come to dinner tomorrow?' 'I'd *love* to' (enthusiastically). The teacher briefly corrects stress and intonation so that students are properly conveying the feeling of the chosen abverb. The two students then come into the room and take turns to ask questions to individual students in the class to do something in the manner of the abverb, for example:

> 'What did you have for breakfast?', 'What's the weather like today?', 'How are you?'

which the class must answer in the manner of the adverb.

When they have guessed the word the class chose, the game is repeated with different students waiting outside and a different adverb selected.

5 Students divide into groups of four. Each group is given two sets of cards which they place in the middle of the table. On one set each card asks students to perform a function.

eg: Apologise to your friend for losing his book / breaking his record / forgetting his birthday

Invite your friend to a party / dinner / go on holiday with you

Complain to your friend that her radio is on too loud / she always arrives late / she forgot your birthday

The other set of cards tell students how to respond:

Answer apologetically / angrily / sarcastically / enthusiastically / irritatedly

Even if the mood is not particularly appropriate, students must think of ways to respond convincingly in the manner written on their card. Student A picks up a card from the first pack and performs the function for example: 'I'm sorry but I've lost the book you lent me'.

Student B picks up a card from the second pack and responds in the manner stated, eg for 'angrily': 'You'll just have to buy me another one then!' Students C and D have to guess the manner written on B's card. If they guess correctly B wins a point for having been convincing. Students repeat the abovein rotation around the group. The student with the most points at the end is the winner.

6 The activity on p28 may be repeated with a tape instead of a text. Here the teacher plays a tape once. Students individually write five things they know for sure from what they have heard. They compare what they have written with a partner and discuss how they know these facts. The tape is then played a second time and students individually write down five things they do not know for sure but which they imagine to be true from what they've heard. Again they compare with a partner. Pairs form groups of four and students in turn read out their lists, with the others in the group trying to decide which part of the extract led to students to their conclusions.

■ **Predictive/Referential Listening** See pp38–41

1 The teacher plays a tape of a passage which has various sentence connectors

eg: but / however / so / since / because / while / although / meanwhile

Students discuss the gist of the tape in pairs and the teacher plays the tape a second time. Students are then given a written transcription of the passage with all the connectors removed, and in pairs they fill in the gaps with the appropriate words. The whole class then discuss, sentence by sentence, which connectors are correct and the teacher plays the tape a final time for students to check their answers with the original.

2 Before playing a taped extract with various sentence connectors included, the teacher writes on the board a list of half sentences about the passage, ending with a connector,

eg: He tried to find his key but ....

She couldn't open the door, so ....

It was raining hard, although..

She thought about her boyfriend while..

Students in pairs discuss what they think the passage will be about. Class discussion follows. Pairs then predict how each of the sentences finishes, and compare their ideas with those of another pair. The teacher then plays the tape and students discuss as a class how close their predictions were.

A general extension of this is for the teacher to play a tape and stop it at moments where it is easy to predict what is going to be said next. Students are asked to write down their predictions before discussing with class and teacher.

3 Pairs of students are each given the same set of multiple choice questions about a taped extract and discuss what they think the extract will be about. Group and class discussion follows. The tape is played. The class comments on how close they think their predictions were.

4 The teacher plays the opening line of a dialogue, stopping the tape before the second speaker responds to the first. Students in pairs discuss what they think the response will be, bearing in mind the mood and attitude of the first speaker as well as the actual words spoken. The teacher then plays the actual response and stops the tape again. Students now comment in pairs as to how close their predictions were, and then proceed to discuss how the first speaker will responds next. Clearly, actual details will not always be possible to anticipate, especially at the beginning of the conversation, but students can make general guesses, such as 'He's going to make an excuse' or 'She isn't going to accept his apology.'

As in the previous activity, this is repeated to the end of the dialogue when students comment as a class on how easy or difficult it was to make such predictions.

5 The teacher plays the introductory part of a radio interview. For example: 'Today we're going to speak to a well-known writer about her latest novel . . .' and stops the cassette. Students in pairs predict the questions the interviewer is going to ask.

The teacher then plays the first question asked, and the response, before stopping the cassette. Students now predict in pairs what the second question will be, bearing in mind what has already been said. This process is repeated to the end of the dialogue when students come together as a class and comment on how easy or difficult it was to predict the direction of the conversation.

6 The teacher plays a series of ten very short taped extracts in which pronouns and substitutes are used to refer back to nouns already mentioned. Before playing the tape she writes a short phrase on the board from each extract, underlining the pronoun:

eg: I'll go <u>there</u> tomorrow.
I saw <u>him</u> yesterday.
The <u>former</u> was very interesting.
<u>She</u> didn't like <u>it</u> much.

The tape is played straight through without stopping and students individually note down what they think each underlined word refers to. They then compare their answers with a partner. The teacher plays the tape a second time, but this time pauses after each to allow students to discuss their answers again. Finally, pairs report their answers to the rest of the class, and if there is disagreement, the teacher plays the relevant extract again and allows students more time to decide.

CHAPTER 5

Paper 5
The Interview

GENERAL DESCRIPTION

The oral interview often takes place on the same day as the Listening Comprehension. This is almost always at a separate time from the three other papers, sometimes before them, sometimes after – and is arranged by the school, college or examination centre in consultation with the Local Examination Syndicate.

The interviewers are appointed on account of their recent experience in teaching English to foreigners. Almost all are in regular contact with foreign learners through their work, so are able to make accurate and reliable assessments of candidates' spoken English. They are usually friendly, approachable and easy to talk to, and their job is to make interviewees feel as comfortable as possible within the formal interview setting.

There is a certain amount of choice as to how the school or centre, in consultation with the candidates, wishes to arrange its interviews. The interviewer may be asked to see one or two candidates at a time. The dynamic of the communication is obviously different according to whether the relationship is one-to-one or one-to-two: if the latter, the examiner can encourage the candidates to talk with each other as well as to herself.

At the end of the interview the examiner completes a printed piece of paper for each candidate. This is then sent to Cambridge to be assessed with the candidate's other papers. The six areas of assessment are: fluency; grammatical accuracy; pronunciation of sentences; pronunciation of individual sounds; interactive communication and vocabulary resource. Candidates are marked on a range of 0–5 for each of the six language skills – 0 meaning virtually no English at all, 5 implying native speaker competence. The marks for each of the six areas are allotted by the interviewer in accordance with these criteria of skills:

1 Fluency

5 Comfortable at natural-speaker speed and rhythm in everyday contexts, though there may be some hesitation when speaking on more abstract topics.

4 In everyday contexts speaks with minimal hesitation. Hesitation when discussing abstract topics but does not demand unreasonable patience of the listener.

3 Does not hesitate unreasonably in everyday contexts though may experience some difficulty with more abstract topics.

2 Unacceptable hesitation even in everyday contexts.

1 Speech very disconnected.

0 Not capable of connected speech.

2 Grammatical accuracy

5 Few if any errors over a wide range of structures, including tenses, prepositions, etc. which are completely sufficient to deal with everyday contexts, and more than adequate for abstract topics.

4 Basic structures sound, though more difficult structures may sometimes be inaccurate.

3 Basic structures sufficiently controlled to deal adequately with everyday contexts though difficulty experienced with more complex structures.

2 Basic structures often inaccurate in everyday contexts. More complex structures rarely attempted or grossly inaccurate.

1 Gross distortion of basic structures.

0 No awareness of basic grammatical functions.

3 Pronunciation: Sentences

5 Fully natural stress-timing, rhythm, and placing of stress, intonation patterns and range of pitch within sentence, natural linking of phrases.

4 Good stress-timing, rhythm, placing of stress, intonation, etc. so that in spite of sounding foreign, speech is easily understood.

3 Stress-timing, rhythm, placing of stress, intonation, etc. noticeably foreign but can mostly be understood.

2 Unacceptably foreign speech patterns predominate, with incorrect phrasing impeding interpretation. Often difficult to understand.

1 Stress and intonation so foreign that little is comprehensible.

0 Not intelligible, through faulty stress and intonation.

4 Pronunciation: Individual sounds

5 All individual sounds virtually correct and recognisable.
4 Individual sounds sufficiently well pronounced for clear and easy understanding.
3 Sounds sufficiently correct for broad understanding.
2 Poor pronunciation of individual sounds
1 Pronunciation so poor that it represents only a crude approximation to English sounds.
0 Unintelligible.

5 Interactive communication

5 Wholly effective at communicating both actively and receptively, both in everyday contexts and on more abstract topics.
4 Communicates effectively in everyday contexts, but lacks natural responsiveness when dealing with more abstract topics.
3 Communication level mainly adequate in everyday contexts, but awkward and non-effective on more unexpected ground.
2 Does not communicate naturally even in everyday contexts.
1 Rarely able to communicate even at a basic level.
0 Understanding and communication minimal.

6 Vocabulary resource

5 Wide and appropriate range of vocabulary for everyday tasks and generally adequate range for discussing more abstract topics.
4 Shows few gaps in vocabulary for everyday tasks though more abstract topics reveal weaknesses.
3 Vocabulary adequate for everyday tasks though may experience difficulty when discussing more abstract topics.
2 Vocabulary often insufficient to accomplish even everyday tasks.
1 Severe lack of vocabulary makes it almost impossible to communicate.
0 Vocabulary too slight for even minimal communication.

The University of Cambridge Local Examinations Syndicate has produced videos showing performance levels in the Interview, which are available from Cambridge. See footnote, p1.

Allthough the marking scheme is complex (the Handbook says that the 'raw' maximum of 30 is scaled to a fine total of 40), 3 is generally considered, in practice, to be the minimum mark to aim at on each section, with 4 suggesting a good pass at that particular oral skill and 2 falling below the required standard. According to the Handbook an adequate (Grade C) mark is about 60 per cent of the total available, ie

18 out of 30 which means that, practically speaking, 6 individual marks of 3 is considered pass standard on this paper.

CONTENTS OF INDIVIDUAL SECTIONS

The interview lasts between 15 and 20 minutes according to the Handbook but perhaps rather less in practice. It consists of four shortish sections. The first is a two or three minute 'warm up' – name, country, job, etc. The remaining three discussion sections are linked by a common theme which is then explored from three different angles. The first is via a picture, the second via a short written text and the third by means of some kind of printed stimulus such as a map, a graph or an advertisement. For example, if 'Work' is the theme the examiner chooses to explore, candidates might be asked to describe a photograph of an office full of people and equipment in the picture section, then given a short paragraph about the monotony of factory life to silently read and discuss before, in the third section, finally looking at an advertisement for temporary work in a restaurant and asked to explain why they would or wouldn't wish to apply for such a job. Instead of the 'Communicative activity' third section of the oral, which could also be a role play of some kind, candidates who have taken the book option can elect to discuss their book with the examiner. Sometimes, in fact, an interviewer is prepared to give over much of the interview to book discussion. Outlines of plot and character, and the candidates' overall feelings and opinions about the book will usually form the subject matter.

BREAKDOWN OF SKILLS NEEDED

In the interview a candidate will need to be able to perform a number of functions in spoken English. These include: describing a picture; giving his opinion on a topic of general interest; answering questions and responding appropriately to the interviewer's comments; putting a short text into his own words; talking about a piece of written information; telling a story; taking part in a role-play; 'translating' diagrammatic representation into words; giving personal information about himself. He will need to carry out these tasks reasonably fluently and with enough vocabulary and grammatical and phonological accuracy to be understood by the examiner.

As important as any linguistic aspects, however, are the candidate's skills of self-presentation, and the way he handles the overall communicative interaction between himself and the interviewer, and, where relevant, himself and other candidates. Throughout oral examination the candidate is in a situation where he must interact with another person or other people. Thus, he will need to understand what is said to him and respond appropriately. He will need to say enough to give the interviewer a clear idea of what he can and cannot do with his English in a conversational setting yet not so much that he delivers a monologue and deprives the examiner or other candidates of the space to make responses and ask questions. The candidate needs a variety of skills other than the purely linguistic, such as sensitivity to the person or people he is with, enough confidence to perform at his best without monopolising the conversation, and the ability to be flexible and adapt to whatever arises. The candidate's personal attributes contribute to how well or badly he comes across. For instance, no matter how good his command of English, he will not do well if he speaks in monosyllables, nor is an interviewer likely to pass him on the Interactive Communication section if she feels she is being lectured at, albeit in perfect English.

Paper 5 is therefore a hybrid of linguistic and psychological factors. With increased confidence comes improved language performance and with improved language performance comes increased confidence. Each is dependent on the other. The next section works on the assumption that the best way to prepare a candidate for the oral examination is to give him as much classroom practice as possible in performing the interview tasks and encouraging him to be receptive to comments made by his teacher and classmates regarding his strengths and weaknesses.

If a candidate opts for the Book option – discussing a previously read set book from a choice of three – the linguistic and psychological factors mentioned above will operate in much the same way.

SUGGESTED CLASSROOM ACTIVITIES

We recommend that the following activities are done more-or-less in sequence during the First Certificate course. Our hope here is that familiarity with the tasks and conversational features of the interview situation will breed confidence at being able to handle them on the day of the oral examination.

Warm-up phase

Students need practice in giving simple information about themselves. The kinds of questions an interviewer will ask in this section may be predicted – 'Tell me something about yourself', 'How long have you been studying English?', general openers, and, according to the candidate's specific situations, so too, are 'How long have you been in England?', 'Have you ever been to England or the USA?', 'What do you do for a living?', 'What would you like to do when you leave school?', 'How often do you speak English?', 'Have you got any brothers or sisters?' etc. Students in groups could predict likely questions and prepare grammatically accurate answers as suitable responses. Pairs could then ask and answer each other's questions and discuss how they think they performed. As long as candidates are made award of the variables which always operate in oral situations, there is no reason why a short written paragraph entitled 'Me' could not be set for homework fairly early on in the course, and, after teacher correction, learned for use in the warm-up section if the opportunity arises.

Describing a picture

1 Students need to be taught the language of picture description. Although not essential in the examination, this can help candidates find their verbal way around a picture. The following words and phrases are particularly useful:

Dealing with topography:

In the top left / right hand corner there's a
In the bottom
In the background / foreground
To the left / right of . . .
above, below, in between, behind, in front of, opposite, next to

Dealing with unclear elements:

The thing at the top looks like . . .
seems to be a / looks as if it / could be

I don't know the name of the thing next to . . .

It's not clear what they're doing . . .
Maybe they're . . . ing
They might be . . . ing

From the expression on her face, I
imagine . . .

I can't make it out exactly . . .
It's a bit blurred / faint, isn't it?

Dealing with 'Now' elements:

Candidates should be taught the correct tense for describing pictures is the Present Continuous, not the Present Simple, as so many foreign learners think. It is wrong, for example, to say 'In this picture two people walk in a park. One of them holds a dog on a lead. The sun shines.' It is correct to say 'In this picture two people are walking in a park. One of them is holding a dog on a lead. The sun's shining.' Large pictures should be available for classroom use so that students can practise oral and written descriptions in the Present Continuous tense. Initially, students could be given a picture with a description beside it where verbs in the Present Continuous have been omitted. They must then supply the missing information in the correct present tense. Here is an example:

In this picture two people – a man and a woman (1)................ shop window. They (2)................ with their backs to us and we can't see their faces. They are an elderly couple, probably husband and wife. The woman (3)................ a light coat and (4)................ the man's arm. The man (5)................ check coat and (6)................ on the woman's left.

Only one or two such gap-fills should be necessary before students are asked to make free descriptions of pictures, but if they persist in using the Present Simple, more gapped exercises could be set.

2 Students work in pairs. Each student is given a different picture. Student A describes her picture to Student B who draws it from the description. After the students have compared the drawn picture with the one given out, they change over, with student A doing the drawing from student B's oral description. Comparison and discussion ensure as before.

3 Students work in pairs. Each student is given the same picture. Student A is asked to think of three or four obvious questions to ask the other about the picture. Student B is asked to think of the three or four most important pieces of information to give his partner about the picture. After about 5 minutes' preparation A asks B his questions and B responds appropriately. Discussion ensues as to how far A and B anticipated the same areas of information. A different picture is handed out, with this time B thinking of questions, and A statement answers.

4 Students need practice moving from factual description of a picture to giving their own experiences of the situation presented in the picture. In the photograph of the elderly couple, for instance, they could be told that the following questions might be used in the transition from one phase to another:

This couple look as if they've been happily married for years. What do you think the advantages (and/or disadvantages) of this kind of relationship are?
or Could this photograph be set in your country? If not, why not?
or Do you think window displays are generally effective advertisements?

Various pictures could then be given out for students to think of these types of questions for themselves. Pairwork could take the place of the picture section, with one student acting as the inverviewer, the other as the candidate. The subsequent discussion amongst pairs would concentrate on the effectiveness of the interviewer's 'opening out' questions – did they enable the candidate to speak, or were they difficult for her to answer? Students in pairs then switch roles and repeat.

5 One student could role-play the 'warm-up' and picture description sections of the interview in front of the class – the teacher acting as interviewer. After five minutes or so the student comes out of role and comments on his performance. If he consents, classmates and teacher also comment in as constructive and encouraging a way as possible. Students may need help making constructive criticism. If the teacher feels this could be problematic she may wish to leave individual student role-play in front of the class until later. On the other hand, if she abandons it altogether, she misses an opportunity to develop her students' communicative sensitivity, critical awareness, language insight, confidence and sense of perspective. Perhaps the most important point here is the student who role-played the candidate should be the first to comment on her performance and if she so chooses, the only one to do so. In practice, the sternest critic is usually oneself others tend to be much more generous.

Reading and discussing a short text

1 After the picture work, students need to be informed that the short text which follows continues the theme of the picture. The interviewer has three texts on three thematic areas suggested by the picture and may ask the candidate to read silently one, two or three of these texts before asking questions to test comprehension of content and sensitivity to style and register. The texts which follow the picture on p106 are the following:

a Mrs Brown is a very nice person. We don't see many people who look like her around here. She's not very tall, but she's quite well-built and plump. She's got green eyes and a turned-up nose. She usually wears her hair in a bun. Her husband is also small and looks out of place in the city.

b Window shopping is my favourite way to spend a Sunday. I can stroll through the town centre without having to fight the crowds, secure in the knowledge that I will not be spending anything. For a couple of hours I can escape into a dream world where I can own anything I want.

c Let me show you our latest model, madam. You can see it's fitted with all the most up-to-date technology, including a Dolby sound system and a cassette-to-cassette recording facility. I am sure you will not be disappointed with what it has to offer.

Initially, the teacher could elicit from students the types of questions the interviewer could ask each one individually, or two or three in comparison. The questions could be written on the board for students to copy. Questions on these particular texts might include the following:

- Describe Mrs Brown to me in your own words
- Why does the writer say that window shopping is her favourite way to spend a Sunday?
- Is this text meant to be written or spoken, do you think?
- Where would you see or hear the third text?
- What do you think the 'model' is?

As with the photographs, questions about the text often lead on to opinions or life experiences,

eg:
- Are you tempted personally by the sales technique used here?
- Have you ever been window shopping?
- What are the advantages and disadvantages of cassettes compared to records?

2 Once students are familiar with sample texts and questions, they could be given other pictures and asked to anticipate the subject matter of the texts which follow on from them. A class 'brainstorming' session seems appropriate here, with the teacher

writing students' ideas on the board. For example, this picture might generate the suggestions beneath it:

Information about a particular mountain – its height and geological composition; the psychology of mountaineering; a weather forecast for a mountainous region; biographical information about a well-known mountaineer; different types of natural scenery; an advertisement for a climbing holiday; accidents in hills and mountains; the importance of appropriate clothing for walking in remote scenery.

The next stage is for students to work in pairs, choose one of the subject areas and write a short text on it, also thinking of questions to test comprehension and encourage discussion. The teacher monitors the English for accuracy before re-forming pairs so that student A reads student B's text and answers his questions, then vice versa.

3 An individual student could role-play the candidate with the teacher as the interviewer. The rest of the class watch, and assess performance and level of English if the student gives his consent.

Participating in a communicative activity

1 Students need first to be informed that in this section they will usually be handed a piece of printed information, and asked to perform a language task in connection with it. The information, thematically connected with the picture and the text, can be in verbal or diagrammatic form – a map, an advertisement, a timetable, a plan of a building, etc. They should also be made aware of the different kinds of activity they could be asked to perform: discussion, role-play, a short talk of explanation or description, problem-solving, telling a story, giving directions, making a choice from a number of alternatives, etc. The picture on p106 led to the following hand-out for students. Suggested alternative activities for the examiner to generate language work from the candidate are also provided:

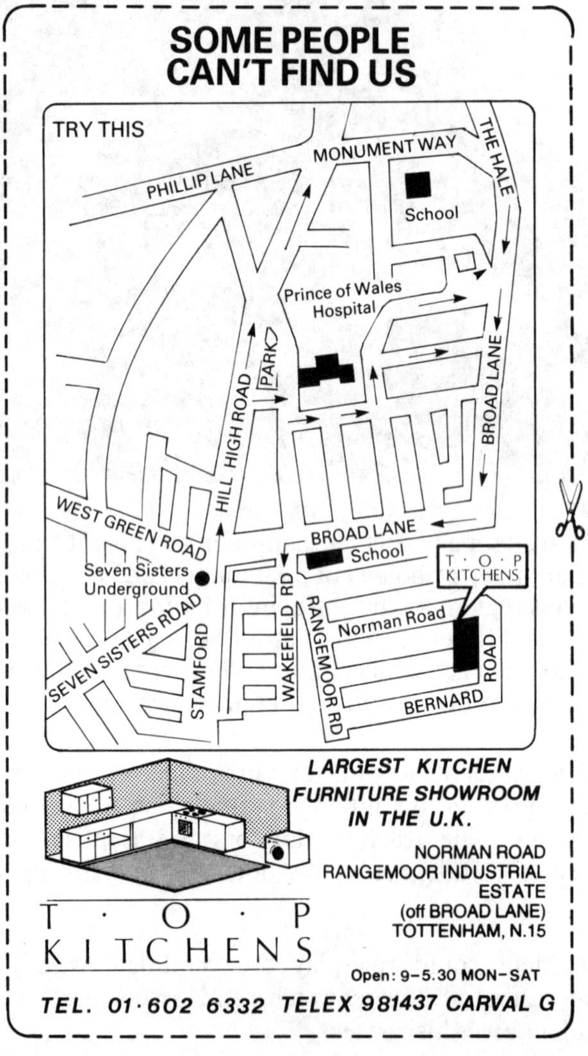

GIVING DIRECTIONS

Hand out map showing kitchen furniture shop. Allow candidate(s) time to absorb the information. Present the following information to the candidate(s):

> You are on the phone talking to a friend who lives in Phillip Lane*. Explain how to get from his house to the kitchen shop in Norman Road by car.

And/or

ROLE PLAY

Assign the following roles to the candidate(s):

1. *First customer:* You want a particular type of cooker for your kitchen. Explain exactly what you are looking for to the assistant.
2. *Assistant:* You do not stock what the first customer requires. Offer an alternative make to the customer.
3. *Second customer:* You have seen what the customer wants in another shop. Interrupt politely and tell the first customer where the shop is.

Allow a suitable period for preparation. Begin the activity in an encouraging and natural manner.

2 Since students need to be acquainted with as many ways of giving information as possible, their first task could be to make a list of the different information-giving formats, then to collect one example of each from newspapers, magazines, stations, estate agents, supermarkets, etc. Obviously, this is easier if students are in an English-speaking country but for those abroad, deciding how to go about acquiring these samples and working on their own initiative to collect them could form a valuable part of their learning process.

3 Once students have acquired a sufficient number of samples, they can work in groups of four to prepare activities for their classmates to carry out. The next stage is for pairs to form, and each student in the pair to take turns at role-playing the interviewer and the candidate in the 'communicative activity' phase of the interview. Class discussion can take place as to whether discursive activities are easier than role-plays, how easy or difficult maps are to decipher, what particular oral activities students hope they will be asked to carry out, etc.

4 Acquainted as they now are with the various oral tasks they may be called on to perform, the students, individually, can be asked to think of the type of 'communicative activity' they hope they are *not* asked to carry out in the examination. The teacher can make a note of each student's particular dislike, then ensure that this is what the student gets as much practice in as possible before his actual interview. Many students find role-play especially difficult. If so, the practice they are getting in role-playing candidate and interviewer across various lesson

*Alternatives for groups: Wakefield Road, West Green Road.

activities suggested for Paper 5 should prove valuable in promoting confidence in this area. In addition, when activity **4** is repeated, the student-as-examiner could make sure he gives his classmate, the student-as-candidate, a role-play in this phase of the interview: both parties will benefit from the experience.

5 As with the other phases, the students should now be in a good position to watch the video of the communication activity, and to make a general assessment of the candidate performance.

6 Alternatively or in addition an individual student role-plays with the teacher in front of the class, as with other sections of the interview process.

The Oral Examination as a whole

By now students should have had enough experience of working on the discrete parts of the interview to take a more global view. Believing as we do that most students have a realistic view of their own language ability – their strengths and weaknesses, as well as that of others – we suggest they should now acquire more detailed practice in assessment. The criteria of skills on pp101–2 need to be made available to them: a lesson could be set aside for the purpose of going through the criteria, possibly using sections of the video to illustrate and exemplify. Complete 10 minute interviews, either simultaneously in pairs or with the teacher interviewing one student in front of the class can now take place on a regular basis. At this stage, the latter has more to offer, for the teacher could 'de-role' at times, asking for the candidate's or class's comments and adding her own. This is an exciting but delicate area, for, as we have seen, the psychological and personality factors affecting attitude and presentation matter almost as much as language areas in the final assessment. Students' sensitivity to these factors inevitably plays a part in class role-play, discussion and assessment: the more a potential FCE interview candidate can successfully anticipate the communicative, interactional aspects of the oral examination *from the examiner's viewpoint* as well as his own, the better he is likely to perform. And, like an actor rehearsing his part for a play, the more practice he has at interview precedure, the more relaxed and confident he is likely to be on the day.

The Set Book option

Up to half the oral examination may be devoted to discussing with the interviewer a set book chosen from three and read beforehand by the candidate. Although this creates extra work for the candidate, he does have the security of knowing the content area of much of the oral examination. He may also write about the book in the Composition Paper.

Classroom activities for the book option would differ little from those above, ie the interview would be role-played with the emphasis on retelling the story, discussing the characters and exploring feelings and opinions about the book.

Before leaving Paper 5, we should like to acknowledge that we have not attempted to make separate suggestions to improve pronunciation and intonation, the only aspect of Paper 5 neither tested elsewhere nor directly concerned with conventional interchange. In our opinion, phonological awareness should be incorporated into almost every lesson as part of the larger whole, bringing a confidence and correctness to students' communicative abilities in a naturally progressive way.